The Leopard Learning Assembly Book

'Steps in the right direction'

WJ and BJ Wilcock

Leopard Learning

Acknowledgements

The authors and publishers would like to thank the following: Mr. Stephen Skepper for his technical assistance; Miss Rachael Smith, member of the British Dragon Boat Racing Association, for information regarding Chinese cultures. Every effort has been taken to ensure that no other author's copyright has been infringed. Should this have inadvertently occurred, the authors and publishers express their sincere regrets and undertake to make appropriate acknowledgements in future editions.

Text © WJ and BJ Wilcock 1998

Illustrations © Leopard Learning 1998

First published by Leopard Learning Ltd, PO Box 2271, Bath, BA2 6RU, 1998

The right of WJ and BJ Wilcock to be identified as the author of this work has been asserted by them in accordance with the Copyright, Designs and Patents Act 1988.

The copyright holders authorise ONLY users of *The Leopard Learning Assembly Book* to make photocopies or stencil duplicates of the copymasters for their own or their classes' immediate use within the teaching context.

No other rights are granted without permission in writing from the publishers or under license from the Copyright Licensing Agency Limited. Further details of such licenses (for reprographic reproduction) may be obtained from the Copyright Licensing Agency Limited, 90 Tottenham Court Road, London W1P 9HE.

Copy by any other means or for any other purpose is strictly prohibited without the prior written consent of the copyright holders. Applications for such permission should be addressed to the publishers.

A catalogue record for this book is available from the British Library.

ISBN 1 8999 29 30 4

Typeset by Leopard Learning Ltd, Bath

Printed in Great Britain by Page Bros; Norwich

To Zoë and Imogen

Foreword

Since my retirement as a head of lower school I have published two books of secondary school assemblies: *Through the Year* (1990) and *One More Step* (1993).

It has been gratifying to see that these books have become widely used in secondary schools. Colleagues in the teaching profession have subsequently asked that I consider writing a similar book of assembly themes for younger children in primary schools. For this purpose I have been fortunate to be able to call upon the advice and expertise of my wife who is a retired primary school teacher.

This joint project we now commend to you in the hope that it will bring fresh ideas to primary school teachers who are called upon to lead school collective worship or take class assemblies and that it will help to provide the children with a grounding in the Christian faith.

W J and B J Wilcock

Contents

Introduction	vi
At-a-glance assembly guide	vii
Thematic index	xi
Assemblies 1-70	1
Prayers	82
Resource sheets	83

Introduction

The Leopard Learning Assembly Book is intended to provide a highly practical, comprehensive assembly resource for busy primary school teachers. It provides:
- 70 complete assemblies which can be used across the whole primary range.
- 27 photocopiable resource sheets which can be used either to support the assemblies as overhead transparencies or for follow up work.
- a short selection of useful prayers.
- a thematic index to enable teachers to use the assemblies as flexibly as possible alongside other work or projects in the school.

The emphasis throughout is upon Christian teaching in order to conform with the regulations of the Education Act. However approximately half the assemblies are suitable for use in multi-faith situations as they follow a moral theme appropriate to all faiths and there is a special section (Assemblies 27-34) which provides specific materials on other faiths and cultures.

Within the book you will find an assembly for nearly every occasion and need:
- 'instant assemblies'
- assemblies for special times of the year
- assemblies of different lengths
- assemblies with stories
- 'interactive' assemblies (often involving the use of the overhead projector if desired)
- assemblies which can be used with either the whole school or with a class
- assemblies which can be linked to topics or curriculum work
- two special assemblies which provide a complete 'off-the-peg' carol service and Nativity play.

The assemblies are intended for use with the whole 5-11 age range. However some focus a little more on the interests of one particular age group (infants or juniors) and you will find reference to this in the 'At-a-glance assembly guide'. You will find that the assemblies at the front of the book provide material structured around the school year; those later on are for more general use.

All the songs and hymns are drawn from the two most popular primary school hymn books, which will be in use in most primary schools. These are: *Junior Praise* published by Marshall, Morgan and Scott, and *Come and Praise*, BBC Publications.

Most of the assemblies require very little preparation; many can be done 'instantly'; a few, for special occasions or performances, are highlighted as requiring thorough preparation. The level of preparation is indicated in the 'At-a-glance assembly guide'. As a general rule we have tried to avoid stipulating very specialist or specialist 'props'.

Approximate timings are given for each assembly, but these are recommendations only - you may find in *your* school that the time you need does vary a bit!

All the assemblies come with prayers, song choices and extensions and curriculum links. Many also come with suggested Bible readings as well.

At-a-glance guide to the assemblies

Those assemblies marked with an asterisk are accompanied by a photocopiable resource sheet.
Those assemblies marked 'S' contain a story.

	Title	Theme/aim and age focus	When to use	Time	Essential Preparation
1	Sand castles* (S)	Good foundations (General/Infant)	Start of school year	8-10 mins	None
2	Blue Peter	Life is fun (General)	Start of school year	8-10 mins	Some
3	Trees*	Thanks for God's gifts (General)	Harvest	8-10 mins	Some
4	Water	Thanking God for rain (General)	Harvest	8-10 mins	None
5	Fireworks	How God wants us to live (General)	November 5	8-10 mins	Some
6	Bonfire night*	Respect for others (General)	November 5	8-10 mins	None
7	Jigsaws	We are all important (General)	Advent	12-15 mins	Some
8	Names	The name of Jesus (General)	Advent	8-10 mins	None
9	Good news	The good news of the Bible (General)	Advent	8-10 mins	Some
10	Robin Red Breast* (S)	We are all important (General)	Advent	8-10 mins	Some
11	The Christmas tree	Christmas customs (General)	Advent	6-8 mins	A lot
12	Footprints*	Following Jesus' example (General)	Advent	6-8 mins	Some
13	Birthdays	Christmas, Jesus' birthday (General)	Advent	8-10 mins	Some
14	The Christmas story*	Nativity play (General/Infant)	Advent	15-20 mins	A lot
15	Carol service*	School carol service (General)	Advent	15-20 mins	A lot
16	Snow*	The wonders of nature (General)	Snowy weather	6-8 mins	Some

	Title	Theme/aim and age focus	When to use	Time	Essential Preparation
17	Snow Tracks*	Setting a good example (General)	Snowy weather	8-10 mins	Some
18	Seeds	Thanking God (General/class assembly)	Spring	6-8 mins	A lot
19	What Ali owes* (S)	Gratitude (General)	Mother's day	6-8 mins	Some
20	April Fools	The wisdom of following Jesus (General)	April 1	8-10 mins	None
21	Hot cross buns	The meaning of Easter (General)	Easter time	6-8 mins	Some
22	Easter eggs*	New life (General/Infant)	Easter time	6-8 mins	Some
23	Pass it on!	Passing on the Good News (General/Infant)	Ascension day	15-18 mins	Some
24	Wind*	God's strength (General)	Whitsuntide Windy days	10-12 mins	None
25	Silhouettes*	Transfer to secondary school (General/Junior)	End of school year	6-8 mins	Some
26	Crabs* (S)	Remembering lessons learned (General)	End of school year	6-8 mins	None
27	Chinese New Year* (S)	Appreciating differences (General/Junior)	Chinese New Year	6-8 mins	Some
28	Guru Nanak's carpet (S)	Caring for God's creatures (General)	General	6-8 mins	Some
29	I can't (S)	God's call to Mohammed and Moses (General/Junior)	General	8-10 mins	Some
30	Dragon boats* (S)	How other people celebrate (General)	General (June)	10-12 mins	Some
31	Festivals of light	Giving thanks for light (General)	General	6-8 mins	Some
32	Chinese lights*	The Chinese festival of light (General)	Spring	6-8 mins	None
33	Diwali	Diwali (General)	Autumn (Diwali)	6-8 mins	None
34	Hanukkah*	Hanukkah (General)	December (Hanukkah)	6-8 mins	Some

	Title	Theme/aim and age focus	When to use	Time	Essential Preparation
35	Christmas light	The Christmas festival of light (General)	Advent	6-8 mins	A lot
36	The Hokey Cokey	Commitment (General)	General	10-15 mins	Some
37	The talking book	God speaks to us (General)	General	10-12 mins	Some
38	Keyholes	To encourage church attendance (General)	General	6-8 mins	Some
39	Hands	Using our talents (General)	General	10-15 mins	Some
40	Fog	Overcoming difficulties (General)	Winter (Foggy weather)	8-10 mins	None
41	Alarms	Right and wrong (General)	General	6-8 mins	Some
42	Remembering	Good memories (General)	General	12-15 mins	Some
43	Luck*	Trusting God (General)	General	6-8 mins	Some
44	Horseshoe nail (S)	Everyone is important (General)	General	6-8 mins	Some
45	New clothes (S)	Thinking of ourselves (General)	General	8-10 mins	None
46	Simon says	Good advice (General/Infant)	General	8-10 mins	None
47	Follow my leader	The best example (General/Infant)	General	6-8 mins	None
48	Traffic signals	When to go, stop or be ready (General)	General	6-8 mins	Some
49	Snakes and ladders*	Life's ups and downs (General)	General	6-8 mins	Some
50	The Lord's prayer	The meaning of the Lord's prayer (General)	General	8-10 mins	None
51	Houses*	The church is God's house (General)	General	8-10 mins	Some
52	Who's job is it?* (S)	Class responsibility (General/Infant)	General	6-8 mins	Some

	Title	Theme/aim and age focus	When to use	Time	Essential Preparation
53	Teddy bears	Jesus is our friend (General/Infant)	General	15-20 mins	Some
54	Listen	Listening to Jesus (General/Infant)	General	6-8 mins	Some
55	Thank you (S)	Gratitude (General)	General	6-8 mins	Some
56	Bullies (S)	Respect for others (General)	General	6-8 mins	None
57	Green cross code (S)	We are valued by God (General)	General	8-10 mins	Some
58	Fast and slow (S)	Taking care (General)	General	6-8 mins	None
59	The Lion's thorn (S)	Kindness is rewarded (General)	General	6-8 mins	None
60	Lion and mouse (S)	Kindness is rewarded (General)	General	6-8 mins	None
61	The crooked man	There is good in the world (General/Infant)	General	6-8 mins	None
62	I spy	Forming good impressions (General)	General	8-10 mins	Some
63	Five pound note	Making promises (General)	General	6-8 mins	Some
64	Badges	Belonging (General/Junior)	General	8-12 mins	Some
65	Hobbies	Reliability and persistence (General/Junior)	General	8-15 mins	Some
66	King Midas* (S)	Greed (General)	General	6-8 mins	None
67	Clocks*	Reliability (General)	General	6-8 mins	Some
68	Red Riding Hood (S)	Don't pretend (General/Infant)	General	6-8 mins	None
69	The rainbow (S)	God's faithfulness (General)	General	6-8 mins	None
70	Keys*	Hard work leads to success (General)	General	6-8 mins	Some

Thematic Index

Animals 22, 26, 27, 28, 58, 59, 60, 68
Bible, Bible stories 1, 14, 15, 29, 37, 50, 55, 56, 69
Advent 7-15, 35
Birds 10, 22
Birthdays 13, 14, 15, 27
Books 9, 37, 62
China (stories and customs) 27, 30, 32
Christmas 7-15, 35
Churches 38, 51
Clothes 45
Communication 2, 23, 37, 48, 50
Diwali 33
Easter 21, 22
Environment 3, 4
Families 14, 15, 22, 68
Festivals *Hanukkah* 34, *Chinese New Year* 27, 30, 32, *Christmas* 7-15, 35, *Diwali* 33, *Easter* 21, 22, *Festivals of light* 31
Food 21, 66
Greece (stories from) 58, 59, 60, 66
Harvest 3, 4
Health education 5, 6, 39, 41, 57,
Hinduism 33
Hobbies 64, 65
Holidays 1, 26
Houses and homes 1, 38, 41, 70
Islam 29
Jesus, stories told by Jesus 1, 8, 12, 13, 14, 15, 35, 50, 53, 55, 84
Judaism 34
Light 5, 6, 25, 31-35, 48
Living things 3, 10, 18, 22, 26, 28, 58, 59, 60
My body, myself (senses) 8, 23, 29, 39, 42, 54, 62
Money 19, 63, 66
Names 8
News 9, 23
Plants 3, 4, 18
Safety 5, 6, 41, 48, 57, 70
Sea 1, 26, 30
Signs and signals 2, 11, 12, 17, 41, 48, 64
Spring 18, 21, 22, 32
Starting the school year 1, 2
Summer 1, 30
Time 13, 27, 67
Toys and games 7, 11, 20, 30, 42, 46, 47, 49, 53
Transport 30, 48, 57
Trees 3, 11, 35
Water 4, 18, 30
Weather 16, 17, 24, 40, 69
Winter 16, 17, 40
Work 19, 52

1 SANDCASTLES 8-10 mins RS1

Aim
To show the children the need for good foundations in their lives; (this is an assembly suitable for the start of the school year after the long summer holidays.)

Preparation
No preparation is required. The following visual aids are optional:
- OHT or copymaster of Resource Sheet 1
- paintings by children of what they did in their summer holidays
- a sandtray and some water

When particularly to use
At the start of the school year

Age focus
General/infant

What did you do during your summer holidays? (*Optional*) Did you do this? Or this? (*Show OHT, copymaster or paintings. Ask children for their accounts of summer.*)

Story
Here is a story about being on the beach during the holidays.

Susan and her little sister had gone to the seaside for their summer holiday. They loved to play on the beach and on the first day of their holiday they made a huge sandcastle. It took them all afternoon to make because they constructed it so carefully. It was magnificent; it had roads, tunnels, towers and walls as part of it.

When Mum told them it was time for tea they were very sorry to have to leave their sandcastle. The following morning they ran down to the beach straight after breakfast to have a look at it, but there was no sign of the castle. It had completely disappeared. Where it had once stood the sand was absolutely smooth! What do you think had happened to the castle? (*Ask for suggestions here.*)

That's right. During the night the tide had come in and the water had washed over the sand making everything smooth and flat again. Their castle had disappeared because it was built on sand and couldn't stand up against the strong sea water. (*Here, for younger children, a small castle could be made in the classroom sand pit. Then a small quantity of water poured over it and the children could watch it disappear.*)

Real castles are built out of slabs of stone or rock and are built on rock so that the wind, the rain and even floods are not able to wear them away. They have good foundations.

Jesus told a story about two men who built houses on different foundations. (*With older children you might like to read the Bible version*). One man was very silly because he built his house on sand so that when the wind blew and the floods came his house was soon washed away. The other man was very wise because he chose a good firm rocky place upon which to build. His house stood firm and safe when the winds and floods came.

If we soon forget what we are taught at school and if we don't follow Jesus' example then our behaviour will make people unhappy. But if we remember what we are taught and take notice of what Jesus tells us so that we can learn how to be helpful and kind, then the things we do will make people happy and our deeds will remain strong and firm as a rock. We too will have firm foundations.

Song choices
'The wise man built his house upon the rock' *(Junior Praise 252)*
'Jesus good above all other' *(Come and Praise 23)*

Prayer
Dear God, help us to be wise in all that we do, to be helpful and kind to other people as Jesus wants us to be, so that we will always be strong, steady and firm like the house that was built upon the rock. Amen

Teacher's reference
Matthew Chapter 7 v 24 to 27

Extensions/curriculum links
- Younger children can experiment themselves with sandcastles and water.
- Science: work on the nature of materials for building e.g. the story of the three little pigs.

2 BLUE PETER

8-10 mins

Aim
To show that life can be both exciting and enjoyable

Preparation
- Prepare a diagram of a Blue Peter flag as shown below or ask the children to draw one.
- *(optional)* obtain a recording of the signature tune for the TV programme;

When particularly to use
At the start of the school year

Age focus
General

(Begin by asking the children to say what are their favourite television programmes.) The most popular children's television programme of all time is surely 'Blue Peter'.

Do you recognise this music? *(Play excerpt if you have it.)*

Do you know why the programme is called Blue Peter? What is a Blue Peter?

Here is a picture of one. *(Show picture.)* It is a blue flag with a large white rectangle in the centre. This flag is flown from the mast of any ship which is about to set sail.

You have all set out on a great adventure through life, so if you were a ship you would be flying the Blue Peter. Perhaps you will now see why the title Blue Peter is such a good one for a children's television programme.

You are on a great journey through Primary School. Before long you will start another journey through Secondary School and so life will go on with new experiences and new adventures.

As you journey through life you may well have problems to face. Things will not always be easy for you, but you must never feel that you are on your own. Your parents will help you with any difficulties you may have. Your school teachers are always ready to help. And there is someone else... Who do you think that might be?

Jesus is the best friend anyone can have and he promises to be with us always. *(Here for older children read the second part of the last verse of Matthew's gospel.)* Jesus said: 'Lo, I am with you always, to the close of the age.'

Song choices
'Be bold, be strong for the Lord God is with you' (*Junior Praise* 14)
'Jesus Christ is here' (*Come and Praise* 26)

Prayer
Lord Jesus, we thank you for being our friend and we ask you to be with us always, keeping us safe and helping us with any difficulties we may have.

Extensions/Curriculum links
- A humanities project on flags, their uses and meanings, within wider topics on communication and signs and symbols (See *The Observer Book of Flags*.)

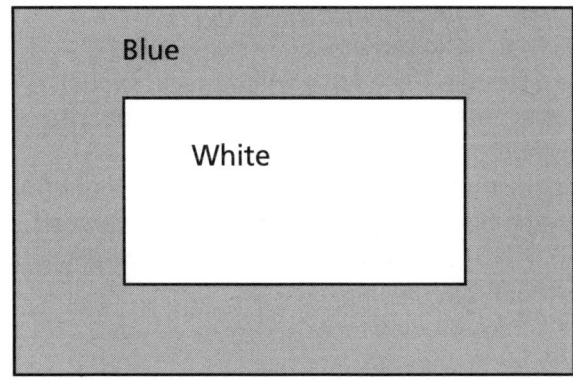

Blue Peter

3 TREES   8-10 mins   RS2

Aim
To encourage a respect for, and an appreciation of, God's world; (this theme is particularly suitable at harvest time or at any time of the year when a class, or the school, is concentrating on growth and the natural world.)

Preparation
You need a display of harvest produce; (*optional*) some pictures of trees or Resource Sheet 2 as an OHT or copymaster.

When particularly to use
Harvest

Age focus
General

What a wonderful display of fruit and vegetables we have here today! At harvest time we thank God for his goodness in supplying us with the food we need.

Today we are going to thank God especially for trees, for they are part of the harvest God provides. Can you name any different types of tree? Here are a few. (*Show OHT or pictures.*)

Why are trees important? (*Encourage the children to make suggestions, along the lines of the following. They could be written on the OHT around the pictures.*)
- Trees help to make the air we breathe much cleaner and stop the soil being blown away by strong winds.
- Trees provide us with wood to make furniture, doors, houses, sheds, fences etc.
- Wood from the trees can be made into pulp in order to make paper - books, drawing paper, writing paper, newspapers, comics, wrapping paper etc.
- The sap from some trees is used to make glue; from other trees the sap is made into rubber.
- Without trees there would be nowhere for some birds to build their nests, and we need the birds to eat the harmful insects which would ruin the crops.
- Trees provide us with delicious fruit to eat. (*Refer to the different types of fruit in the harvest display. Say which grow on trees.*)
- The leaves which fall from the trees in the autumn form into rich compost which is needed to put goodness back into the ground.
- Trees make our world a very beautiful place. Let us quietly think for a few moments what the world would be like if there were no trees. (*Mention here any topical programme of conservation.*)

Prayer
Thank you Heavenly Father for the beauty of the world you have made. Especially today we thank you for trees, for their usefulness and for the pleasure they give. Help us to care for the wonderful world you have made and not to do anything which might spoil it. Thank you for all your gifts of food at harvest-time. May your blessing be upon the elderly people who are going to receive these harvest gifts. Amen

Reading
(*For older pupils*) Psalm Chapter 24 v 1 to 6

Song choices
'All things bright and beautiful' (*Junior Praise* 6, *Come and Praise* 3), 'God who made the earth' (*Junior Praise* 63, *Come and Praise* 10)

Extensions/Curriculum link
- This theme could be presented in conjunction with a project on trees - the different types and how they grow - within science or geography.

4 WATER

8-10 mins

Theme
Thanking God for the rain; this theme is ideal for harvest time or alongside a class topic on water

Preparation
The assembly can be done without preparation. The following visual aids are optional:
- An OHT on which to write children's suggestions.
- Pictures of rivers, lakes or other water sources painted by children beforehand.

When particularly to use
At the start of the school year

Age focus
General

Have you ever made arrangements to go out to play with friends and when the time came it was raining so you couldn't go? Were you cross?

Have you ever been to the seaside when it has been raining and not been able to play on the sands? Were you disappointed?

You may have heard grown-ups grumbling about the weather. What did they say?
> 'It seems to have been raining for days!'
> 'It always rains when I want to do the gardening!'
> 'Whenever I start to clean the car it starts to rain!'
> 'It always rains when I go on holiday!'

Do you think it would be better if it never rained? Let's think for a few minutes what the world would be like if there was no rain. (*Invite suggestions along the lines of the following. They can be written up on the OHT.*)

- We would have no water to drink. But couldn't we drink lemonade?
- We would have no milk because the cows need water to produce milk.
- There would be no orange juice because the trees need to take water from the ground to produce oranges.
- We would be unable to wash to keep ourselves clean.
- The trees would die.
- The crops would not grow.
- There would be no rivers and therefore no lakes or seas. We would have no fish to eat.
- The whole world would become like a huge desert without any life at all.

How fortunate we are that God sends us rain. How grateful we should be - even when it rains when we don't want it to rain.

(*Optional*) Let's have a look at some of the pictures you have painted. They all show either a river, lake or the sea.

Reading
Psalm 104 v 10 to 13

Prayer
Thank you God for sending us the rain, for providing us with water to drink. Help us never to waste the good gifts you provide. Amen

Song choices
'We plough the fields and scatter' (*Junior Praise* 267)
'Water of Life' (*Come and Praise* 2)
'Can you be sure that the rain will fall?' (*Come and Praise* 31)

Extensions/Curriculum links
- Humanities project on weather.
- Art lessons in which the children produce pictures of river views, lakes etc.
- Watering/not watering plants. What happens?

5 FIREWORKS 8-10 mins

Theme
The sort of people God wants us to be; (this assembly is ideal for use around November 5.)

Preparation
- Provide a blank OHT or flipchart sheet to write on.
- (Optional) A poster advertising fireworks, or actual fireworks, either 'live' or old cases; (if live fireworks are to be shown they should be kept in a tin box)

When particularly to use
Near November 5

Age focus
General

Who can tell me what is special about November 5th? What sort of things will you be doing on November 5th? (*Ask for suggestions.*)

Fireworks are fun but they can be very dangerous. We must all be very careful to keep to the rules because sadly every year someone gets hurt, usually because they have done something silly.

What *are* the rules we must obey? (*Write the rules on an OHT or flipchart from children's suggestions, including the following.*)
- Only adults should set off fireworks.
- Stand well clear.
- Don't hold a lighted firework in your hand unless it clearly says you may do so.
- Never pick up a firework which seems to have gone out.
- Keep all fireworks in a tin box.
- Don't wear Wellington boots or other loose clothing where fireworks may get caught.

Tell me what are your favourite fireworks. What do they do? (*Children give suggestions.*)

Have you noticed that fireworks seem to fit into two different groups? There are fireworks which make a lot of noise, which splutter or explode or shoot up into the air. (*Show pictures or actual examples - empty cases could have been kept from the previous year.*)

Then there are beautiful fireworks which sparkle or which fill the night sky with beautiful colours giving light and pleasure to everyone.

I think that people, even boys and girls, are a bit like fireworks. There are those who always make a lot of noise, who splutter and shout and who explode in a fit of temper when something goes wrong.

Then there are people who are kind, helpful and who quietly get on with their work. These people set such a good example that it is as though their lives are shining like lights, helping others to see more clearly how they should live.

I hope you will be very careful on November 5th, and that you will try hard to be like sparkling fireworks that give pleasure to everyone.

Reading (for older children)
In our reading today Jesus tells his followers that they must shine as lights in a dark world. (*Read Matthew Chapter 5 v 14 to 16.*)

Prayer
Lord, help us to be the sort of people you want us to be, helpful, kind, loving and friendly, that our lives may be a good example for others to follow, as though we were lights shining in the darkness. Amen

Song
'Colours of Day' (*Junior Praise* 28, *Come and Praise* 55)

Extensions/Curriculum links
- Design 'care with fireworks' posters.
- Topic on light.

6 BONFIRE NIGHT

8-10 mins   RS3

Aim
To encourage respect for other people

Preparation
None, but the following are optional:
- A Guy Fawkes made before the assembly or OHT or copymaster of Resource Sheet 3

When particularly to use
Near November 5th

Age focus
General

It will soon be bonfire night! Of course fireworks and fires are great fun but they can also be very dangerous. You should only go to a bonfire with an adult. Do you remember these rules?
- Only adults should set off fireworks.
- Stand well clear.
- Don't hold a lighted firework in your hand unless it clearly says you may do so.
- Never pick up a firework which seems to have gone out.
- Keep all fireworks in a tin box.
- Don't wear Wellington boots or other loose clothing where fireworks may get caught.

What do you like especially about bonfire night? The fire being lit? Spectacular fireworks? Jacket potatoes? Treacle toffee? Making a Guy Fawkes?

Here is a Guy Fawkes. (*Show the visual aid of Guy Fawkes at this point.*)

This Guy Fawkes will be placed on top of a bonfire on bonfire night and burned. Isn't that a strange thing to do? Let me explain why it is done.

The original Guy Fawkes was a man who lived nearly four hundred years ago. He didn't like what the leaders of the country were doing so he decided to blow up the Houses of Parliament in London. Fortunately his plot was discovered before he had time to put it into action. Ever since, people have burnt a pretend Guy Fawkes on bonfire night.

It is sad and wrong that people like Guy Fawkes try to bully others into doing what they want them to do. Nobody likes bullies. It is much better to try to persuade people by talking to them.

Prayer
O God we pray today for the leaders of our country that they may be wise in all they decide to do. Help us to be patient when we don't like what other people may be doing. Show us that it is wrong to try to bully them. Rather, help us to try to persuade them to do what we think is best. Amen

Song choices
'When I needed a neighbour were you there' (*Junior Praise* 275, *Come and Praise* 65)
'Make me a channel of your peace' (*Junior Praise* 161, *Come and Praise* 147)

Extensions/Curriculum links
- Historical research into the Guy Fawkes' story.
- Use the resource sheet to stimulate creative writing.

7 JIGSAWS

12-15 mins

Aim
To show that we are all important.

Preparation
You need a jigsaw in a box, another in a bag without its box and a flipchart sheet or blank OHT. With a class or small group, each child could have been asked to bring in one of their own jigsaws.

When particularly to use
Advent

Age focus
General

How many of you like doing jigsaws? (*Show a jigsaw or ask the children to show the ones they have brought in.*) Let's have a look at the ones you have brought in. (*Briefly describe some.*) Some jigsaws are more difficult to do than others. It depends largely on how many pieces there are but also on how complicated the picture is.

How would you set about doing a jigsaw? (*You could write the suggested steps on the OHT.*)
1. Put all the pieces on the table and turn them the right way up.
2. Study the picture very carefully.
3. Find the four corner pieces and put them in place.
4. Collect all the pieces with straight edges and complete the four sides of the jigsaw.
5. Look at the picture again and then sort out the pieces which look to be part of, say, the house, the horse, the soldier, the racing car or whatever the picture is about.
6. Next you could collect together the pieces which look as though they could be sky or grass etc.

When the last piece goes in place you will feel you have done something really good and will feel well-pleased with yourself.

How do you think you would feel if you discovered at the end that there were one or two pieces missing? Sad? Disappointed? Annoyed?

(*Show the jigsaw without the box.*) Here is a jigsaw. Somehow the box has been lost and so we have no pattern or picture to follow. Would it be difficult to do?

As we go about our tasks day by day it is good for us to have patterns or examples to follow. We could try to follow the good example set by our friends, older brothers or sisters and our parents. Jesus, too, came to set us an example and to show us how to live. His is the best example of all to follow.

Every piece of a jigsaw is important. If there are one or two pieces missing the whole picture will be spoiled. In the same way every person in our form (*class, school, Sunday school etc.*) is equally important. If just one person is missing or doesn't behave properly it spoils it for everyone else.

Particularly as Christmas time draws near we thank God for sending Jesus, the best example of all.

Reading for older children
Our reading today tells us that everyone is an important member of God's family. Like a jigsaw we all fit together and work together to do our Heavenly Father's will. (*Read Ephesians 4 v 15 and 16.*)

Carol choices
'Once in Royal David's city' (*Junior Praise* 185)
'Come and praise the Lord our King' (*Come and Praise* 21)

Prayer
Thank you God that each one of us is important to you. As we grow up, help us to follow and copy the example set by Jesus, that we may grow to be more like him. Amen

Extensions/Curriculum links
• Technology project: children designing and making own jigsaws.

8 NAMES

8-10 mins

Theme
Jesus - the best name of all

Preparation
There are several ways of presenting this theme:
- Use the names quoted below as examples. This would not require any preparation.
- Research the meaning of some of the names of the children in the assembly and use these. This could involve a visit to the local library. (See 'Useful resources' below.)
- Use the theme as a class project, each child being asked to discover the meaning of his/her name. This information could be written on cards for a class display.

When particularly to use
Advent

Age focus
General

Did you know that everyone's name has a special meaning? Here are the meanings of some popular names. This is what we have found out. (*Read out some of the names on the list below or alternatively each child could be invited to read out the meaning of his/her own name.*)

I hope there will not be any quarrels about whose name is best. I think they are all very good, attractive names. Your parents chose your names for you not because of the meaning. It is more likely they gave you your special name either because they liked the sound of it or because they have a good friend or relative who already has the same name.

Name	Meaning	Name	Meaning
Adam	red earth	Jessica	God is looking
Adele	noble	Joe	he shall add
Andrew	manly	Karen	pure
Ann(e)	grace	Kenneth	handsome
Barry	looking straight at the mark	Linda	of the ash tree
Beatrice	bringer of joy	Margaret	a pearl
Daniel	whom God has judged	Mark (Marcus)	from the God of war
Diana	Goddess	Paul	small
Edward	wealthy protector	Peter	stone or rock
Emma	maid of the nation	Philip	fond of horses
Gemma	precious stone	Rachael	ewe
George	farmer	Rosaline	fair as a rose
Gregory	watchman	Ruth	vision of beauty
Guy	leader	Sarah	princess
Gwen	white-browed	Stuart	a steward
Helen	light	Susan	a graceful white lily
Howard	sword-guardian	Vivian	alive
Imogen	like her mother	Wendy	wanderer
Jane	grace of the Lord	William	helmet of strength
		Zoe	life

There should never be any argument as to whose name is best because there is one name which is above every name. Can anyone think of this name? It is the name 'Jesus'. His name means 'Saviour of the World'. Paul said: 'there is a name which is above every other name for at the name of Jesus every knee should bow'.

In the Christmas story the angel appeared to Joseph and told him that Mary would have a son and that they should call him Jesus 'for he shall save his people from their sin'.
(*Matthew Chapter 1 v 20 & 21*.)

Prayer
We thank you for our names, Heavenly Father, and that you know us all by name because you love us and care for us. Above all we thank you for Jesus our Friend and Saviour. Amen

Song choices
'Jesus loves me! This I know' (*Junior Praise 140*) 'Jesus, name above all names' (*Junior Praise* 141)
(*For older children*) 'At the name of Jesus' (*Come and Praise* 58, *Junior Praise* 13)

Useful resources
The following books are useful: *Discovering Christian Names* by S. M. Jarvis,
ISBN 0 852631898
Naming Baby by Eugene Stone,
ISBN 0 706310519

Extensions/Curriculum links
- Research on names can be done after the assembly.
- Stories can be written around individual names and their meanings.

9 GOOD NEWS — 8-10 mins

Aim
To show that the Bible contains good news; this assembly is particularly suitable for advent.

Preparation
Obtain a *Good News* Bible; you may also like to have a blank OHT.

When particularly to use
Advent

Age focus
General

If I were to say to you that I have 'Good News' for you, what do you think I might mean? (*Invite suggestions from the children and make a list which may be similar to the following. These can be written on the blank OHT if you like.*)
- We are to have an extra day holiday this Christmas?
- We are going to the theatre to see a pantomime?
- We are going to have a super Christmas party?
- (*Name of pop star or sporting hero*) is coming to our school tomorrow.
- Our class has been chosen to sing Christmas carols on the television.

You may feel that any of those ideas would be good news. As a matter of fact we will soon be having a super Christmas party but the 'Good News' I bring is quite different. It is the good news that God loves us all so much that he sent his son Jesus to be born as a baby at Christmas time and that he came to be our friend (Saviour). This is the story which can be found in the Bible. No wonder the Bible I am going to read from is called *The Good News Bible*.

Reading
Luke Chapter 2 v 8 to 16

Prayer
Dear God we thank you this Christmas time for the good news of the birth of your son Jesus. We thank you that he came to be our friend. Help us to be his friends as we try day by day to be more like him. Amen

Carol choices
'While shepherds watched their flocks by night' (*Junior Praise* 285)
'Go tell it on the mountain' (*Come and Praise* 24)

Extensions/Curriculum links
- Look for positive, 'good news' stories in the papers.
- Produce a good news newspaper article about Jesus' birth.

10 ROBIN RED BREAST
8-10 mins — RS4

Aim
To show that we are all important in God's sight

Preparation
Obtain a Christmas card with a picture of a robin or use Resource Sheet 4 as an OHT or copymaster.

When particularly to use
Advent

Age focus
General

Introduction
Have you ever wondered why so many Christmas cards have pictures of robins like this one? *(Show Christmas card or robin visual.)* What has a robin to do with Christmas? There is a lovely story which gives us a possible reason but it is a 'made-up' story. Here it is.

Story
It was a cold winter's night when Jesus was born. Mary and Joseph had to stay the night in a stable with the animals. Mary had placed the baby Jesus in a trough from which the cattle had eaten their food. Though Joseph had lined the trough with comfortable clean straw the stable was still bitterly cold. The small fire had nearly gone out and Mary was worried that her baby would catch cold so she turned to the animals and asked for their help. She asked the ox first to blow on the embers of the fire to make them burn again but the ox lay fast asleep. Next she asked the donkey but he did not hear - neither did the horse nor the sheep.

Suddenly Mary heard a fluttering of little wings. Looking up she saw a tiny, plain brown robin flying round the stable. The robin had heard Mary ask the other animals to help and was sad that they had not bothered. So he went over to the fire, which by now had nearly gone out, and began to flap his wings. The draught he made caused the fire to come back to life. With his beak he picked up some fresh dry sticks and dropped them on to the fire. Soon the stable became cosy and warm. So intent was the little robin on his task that he hardly noticed that the flames had burned the feathers on his chest making them bright red in colour.

Mary thanked and praised the little robin for all he had done and promised that he would always be remembered for his kind deed. And to this day the robin is known as the Robin Red Breast.

Although that story was made up it does tell us something that is very important. The robin must have felt very small and unimportant when he looked at all the big animals, but it was he who was able to help.

You may feel that you are too small to be important but we all can play our part in making our school a happy place. After all, Jesus himself said that children were the most important people. *(See Matthew Chapter 18 v 1 to 6.)*

Prayer
Father God, it is good to know that you made this wonderful world in which we live and that you have given us life to enjoy. It is even more wonderful to know that you love us and care for us because we are important to you. Help us all to work together to make our school and our homes happy places to be in. Amen

Carol choices
'Little Jesus sweetly sleep' *(Most carol sheets)*
'Away in a manger' *(Junior Praise* 12)

Extensions/Curriculum links
- Investigating other stories about animals or birds who have helped.

11 THE CHRISTMAS TREE   6-8 mins

Aim
To show the significance of some Christmas customs

Preparation
This assembly is centred around putting up and decorating a Christmas tree so preparation is required. You need:
- A Christmas tree
- Obtain, or get children to make, the following decorations: an angel, a snowflake, a star, a robin, a lantern, a Christmas bell, some wrapped boxes as gifts.

When particularly to use
Advent

Age focus
General

It is now time for us to put up our school (class) Christmas tree. Today we are going to begin putting the decorations on it. As we do so I want to tell you why we use these decorations. (*Alternatively a group of children could be rehearsed to place each item on the tree and read the script.*)

1 *Angel* First of all, right at the top of our tree we place an angel. This reminds us that the angel Gabriel told Mary that she would have a very special baby son.

2 *Snowflake* Snow, icicles, silver tinsel - all these give our tree a beautiful wintry appearance. We do this because the church celebrates Christmas, the birthday of the Lord Jesus, in the middle of winter, on December 25th.

3 *Star* The wise men and the shepherds were guided by a star to where the baby Jesus had been born by. So now we place a star on our tree.

4 *Robin* Next we have a robin. We heard the story of the robin and how it got its red breast in our last assembly. (*If you did Assembly 10 last time.*)

5 *Lantern* The lantern reminds us that the baby Jesus would become the light of the world showing people how to come to God's heavenly kingdom.

6 *Christmas bell* At Christmas time the bells ring out, telling of the birth of Jesus. We too must tell others this good news - that God loves us so much that he sent his son Jesus into the world.

7 *Gifts* Lastly we put some decorative gift boxes on our tree. We all like to be given presents at Christmas. But we should also enjoy choosing presents to give to other people. The first Christmas presents were those given by the shepherds and the wise men to the baby Jesus.

During the next few days we will add more decorations to our tree.

Prayer
We thank you Lord for this lovely time of the year when we are getting ready for Christmas, when you came into the world to be born as a tiny baby in the stable at Bethlehem. As the shepherds and wise men brought their gifts to you so we would like to give you our gifts - our love and our grateful thanks. Amen

Carol choices
'Away in a manger' (*Junior Praise* 12)
'Ding dong merrily on high' (*Junior Praise* 38)
'The Holly and the Ivy' (*Come and Praise* 119)

Extensions/Curriculum links
- Research into the customs of Christmas.
- Making and decorating class trees.

12 FOOTPRINTS   6-8 mins   RS5

Aim
To show that Jesus' example is the best one to follow

Preparation
Footprints picture (Resource Sheet 5) as an OHT or a photocopy

When particularly to use
Advent

Age focus
General

(*Show the footprints picture.*) Do you recognise these? What are they? Where are you likely to see footprints like these?

If there had been a fresh fall of snow during the night then, when you start to walk to school next morning you would leave behind you footprints like these.

The next time you go to the seaside, wait until the tide has gone out then run on to the sands. The footprints you leave behind will be just like these.

How many of you know the carol 'Good King Wenceslas'? It tells the story of a king who took his young servant, a page, out into the snow in order to bring help to an old man he had seen gathering firewood. It was very hard to walk in the snow so King Wenceslas told the young lad to follow him and to put his smaller feet into the footmarks the king had made. This made it much easier for him to walk. So the young boy followed in his master's steps.

We, too, should follow in the steps of someone else. We may try to be like our parents or an older brother or sister and in this way we are following in their footsteps. The person who gives us the best example to follow is Jesus. We should try to be like him as we follow in his steps. Jesus says: 'Follow me!' (*See Matthew Chapter 4 v 19.*)

Prayer
Lord Jesus, you are the best example for us to follow for you have shown us how to be loving, kind and helpful. Help us, as we grow up, to become more like you. Amen

Carol choices
'Good King Wenceslas' (*Most carol sheets*)
'The Journey of Life' (*Come and Praise* 45)
'I am planting my feet' (*Come and Praise* 103)

Extensions/Curriculum links
- Research into animal tracks.
- Creative writing about 'tracks in the snow'.

13 BIRTHDAYS

8-10 mins

Aim
To encourage the children to remember that we only have Christmas because it is Jesus' birthday

Preparation
Obtain a birthday card and a Christmas card.

When particularly to use
Advent

Age focus
General

How many of you enjoy having a birthday? Tell me what usually happens on your birthday. I expect you get lots of birthday cards like this one. (*Show card.*) You will probably be given birthday presents as well. You may well have a birthday party with lots of nice things to eat, lots of exciting games and so on. Everyone will sing 'Happy Birthday' especially for you.

How many of you have your birthday in December? Which date in December? There is one special birthday coming up. Who can tell me whose it is? It is on December 25th. This will be the birthday of Jesus. God loved us so much that he sent Jesus to be born as a tiny baby in a manger in order that he might come into the world to teach us about God and eventually to give himself for our sakes.

If December 25th had not been Jesus' birthday then we would not have any cause to celebrate Christmas.

I hope you will remember this Christmas that it is Jesus' birthday and thank God for sending him to be our Saviour. Wouldn't it be a good idea to sing Happy Birthday to Jesus?
> Happy birthday to you,
> Happy birthday to you,
> Happy birthday dear Jesus,
> Happy birthday to you.

No doubt you will all be receiving and sending Christmas cards to each other. These are really Jesus' birthday cards.

Reading
Read Luke Chapter 2 v 1 to 7 in *The Good News Bible*.

Prayer
Thank you Father God for loving us so much that you sent Jesus into the world to be born at Christmas time. Help us always to be grateful for your love and help us to be loving and kind to each other. Amen

Carol choices
- 'Away in a manger' (*Junior Praise* 12)
- 'Love came down at Christmas' (*Most carol sheets*)
- 'Silent Night' (*Junior Praise* 219)
- 'Come and praise the Lord our King' (*Come and Praise* 21)

Extensions/Curriculum links
- Making Christmas cards/birthday cards for Jesus.

14 CHRISTMAS STORY — 15-20 mins — RS6

Aim
To tell the Christmas story in the form of a class nativity play

Preparation
- Thorough preparation and rehearsal is required using the photocopiable play script Resource Sheet 6.
- The cast is as follows: Narrator, Mary, Joseph, Inn keeper, Innkeeper's wife (non-speaking), Three shepherds, Three wise men, The Angel Gabriel, Choir of angels

When particularly to use
Advent

Age focus
General/infant

15 CAROL SERVICE — 15-20 mins — RS7

Aim
To provide a complete school carol service

Preparation
Pupils will have to rehearse thoroughly in order to speak clearly and slowly. The service is set out in photocopiable form for use in school on Resource Sheet 7.

When particularly to use
Advent

Age focus
General

16 SNOW

6-8 mins RS8

Aim
To help the children appreciate the wonders of nature; (this assembly is particularly suitable during a snowy or very cold period at school.)

Preparation
You need an OHT or copymaster of Resource Sheet 8 showing a snowflake. Paintings or models of snowmen made by children before the assembly can also be used.

When particularly to use
Snowy weather

Age focus
General

Introduction
Whenever two British people meet in the street the first thing they always seem to talk about is the weather. This is because in our country we get so many different kinds of weather and it never seems to stay the same for very long. There are certain types of weather which no one likes, such as strong winds which do so much damage, fog which makes it difficult for us to find our way about, and extreme cold. At this time of year we may expect snow - and people have different opinions of snow, as you will hear.

'I don't like the snow', said Grandma, 'because it means I am not able to go out to the shops. The pavements become very slippery and I am afraid of falling.'

'I hate the snow!' Dad said. 'Whenever it snows I am late for work because the cars can only travel very slowly. I'm always afraid of skidding on icy roads.'

'I love the snow," said Mum. 'It makes the countryside look very beautiful when everything is clean and white.'

'I love the snow', said Tim, aged 8, 'because I can go out to play on my toboggan. It's great fun.'

'I love the snow', said Susan, the youngest member of the family, 'because we can all go out into the garden and build a huge snowman.'

(*Optional*) Here is a picture of snowmen like the one that Susan built. (*Show pictures or models.*)

Do you like the snow? Why? Who doesn't like the snow? Why not? (*Record the reasons why children do or do not like the snow on the OHT if you like.*)

Although we have good fun playing in the snow we should always take care not to upset elderly people who may be worried by it. Don't throw snowballs near old people. Don't make slides in the snow where old people are likely to walk.

Everyone agrees that snow looks beautiful even if they don't like going out in it. Have you ever thought what a single snowflake looks like? This is a hugely enlarged picture of a snowflake which shows what it actually looks like. (*Show picture.*) You will see what an amazing pattern it is. Each snow flake is a beautiful and different design. The world of nature is a very wonderful thing, full of extraordinary things.

God shows us even in the shape of a tiny snow flake how much he cares for the world he has made.

Prayer
Father God, we thank you for the enjoyment we have as we play in the snow. Thank you for the beauty of the world you have made.

Although we may enjoy the snow, help us also to be thoughtful and helpful towards elderly people who may be afraid of falling when they have to go out in the snow. Amen

Carol choices
'In the bleak mid-winter' (*Carol sheet*)
'See amid the winter's snow' (*Junior Praise* 213)
'He gave me eyes so I could see' (*Come and Praise* 18)

Extensions/Curriculum links
- Creative writing about snowmen based on the ideas collected on the OHT.
- Create symmetrical artwork or models based on the structure of snowflakes.

17 SNOW TRACKS *8-10 mins* RS9

Aim
To show that wherever we may go people will see and remember us; (this assembly is particularly suitable for a snowy period at school.)

Preparation
You need an OHT or copymaster of Resource sheet 9; alternatively you could get a group of children to copy the tracks on each part of the copymaster onto different sheets of paper.

When particularly to use
Snowy weather

Age focus
General

In winter when it snows the world looks different, doesn't it? One of the lovely things about snowy days is the way that you can see tracks in the snow and try to work out who made them.

Imagine that we have just had a heavy fall of snow. It has now stopped snowing and you have to go across the playground. As you walk across, what will you leave behind you, in the snow? You will leave footprints or tracks rather like these. (*Show top part of OHT or copymaster.*)

What do you think could have made these other marks in the snow? (*Show the remaining parts of the pictures, piece by piece.*)

The answers are:
1. One person walking in the snow
2. An adult walking with a small child
3. An adult pushing a pram
4. A sleigh
5. A child riding a three wheeler bicycle

The last one was more difficult, wasn't it?

If ever we go out into the snow we always leave our marks, footprints, behind us. This shows other people that we have been there.

Wherever we go we are remembered by the people we meet and in that way we make our mark. They may remember we have been there because we have been untidy, badly behaved or ill-tempered. I hope they will remember you because you have been kind, cheerful, friendly and helpful. If you behave like this you will leave behind happy memories, a good impression. We all need to leave good 'tracks in the snow'.

Prayer
Father God, wherever we go help us to be kind and helpful, loving and thoughtful, so that other people will feel happy because we have been there. Amen

Song choices
'One more step along the world I go' (*Junior Praise* 188, *Come and Praise* 47)

Extensions/Curriculum links
- Research, and make a wall display, on animal tracks.

18 SEEDS

6-8 mins

Aim
To show that we should be thankful to God for his wonderful world.

Preparation
(This will need to be done in a science lesson or as a class project prior to the assembly.) The following equipment will be needed: a packet of flower seeds suitable for quick germination (such as marigolds or snapdragons), one 'Jiffy' seed pot for each member of the class, one plant label for each pupil; sufficient potting/seed compost.
The children should fill their plant pots with the prepared compost, then plant three seeds in each pot, well-spaced out. They should write the name of the flower and their own names on the label, inserting them into the pots. The pots should be given a final watering and be placed on the classroom window ledge.
You should explain that, having carried out the instructions on the seed packet, the first signs of life, in the form of tiny green shoots, should appear in the allotted time.

When particularly to use
Spring

Age focus
General

(Begin by recalling how the seeds were planted.)

Our tiny green shoots are now beginning to force their way through the compost. When the plants are large enough you will be able to take them outside to plant them in the school garden, but if you prefer, those of you who have gardens may take them home. We can then expect, in a further... weeks time, that the first flowers will come out. When that happens and we see lovely flowers like the ones shown on the seed packet who should we thank?

First of all there are the people who gathered the tiny seeds and put them into the packets. We have them to thank!

Then, of course, there were the people in the garden centre who sold us the seeds and the compost. If it wasn't for them we would not have been able to grow the flowers. You may also think that I had a hand in it because I brought the seeds into school and showed you how to plant them. And then, you yourselves played a large part because you had to do all the work planting the seeds and making sure that the plants were watered regularly.

Important though they are, all these people could not have made even one beautiful flower if it were not for the kindness of God himself. It is he alone who provides the seeds and brings them to life in the first place. It is he who provides the warmth of the sun and the refreshing rain which make all plants grow. Let us thank God for his love in providing plants which give beautiful flowers for our gardens and homes.

Prayer
For the beauty of the earth, for each tiny bud and flower, for sunshine and rain which you give to make each plant grow, we give you our thanks Heavenly Father. Amen

Song choices
'All things bright and beautiful' *(Junior Praise 6, Come and Praise 3)*
'For the beauty of the earth' *(Junior Praise 48, Come and Praise 11)*
'Stand up, clap hands' *(Junior Praise 225)*

Reading for older children
Matthew Chapter 6 v 26 to 31 *(New International Version)*

Extensions/Cross-curricular links
Follow up the development of the planted seeds week by week on a chart.
Experiment with different growing variables for plants (light, heat, water).

19 WHAT ALI OWES

6-8 mins · RS10

Aim
Showing that people are grateful

Preparation
You need two 'bills' (Resource sheet 10) as OHTs, copymasters or just written on large pieces of paper.

When particularly to use
Near Mother's Day

Age focus
General

This a story about a young boy named Ali who desperately needed some extra pocket money and thought he had a good idea how be could get it. He decided to present his mother with a bill for all the extra jobs he had done around the house.

When Ali's mother came downstairs the following morning she saw the bill, like this one, (*show picture of first bill*), on the breakfast table and read it:

MUM OWES ALI
1. For keeping his bedroom tidy. 40p
2. For cleaning his own shoes. 40p
3. For doing his piano practice. 80p
4. For washing his hands and face everyday. 80p
5. For being good. (Most of the time.) 60p
   Total £3.00

That was a brilliant idea, thought Ali - and it worked. When Ali went to sit down at the table there were three pound coins!

But there was also a folded piece of paper. Ali wondered what on earth it could be and he opened it cautiously. It was another bill, this time from his mother and it read:

ALI OWES MUM
1. For preparing all his meals. NOTHING
2. For doing all the housework. NOTHING
3. For taking Ali on holiday. NOTHING
4. For buying him new clothes. NOTHING
5. For nursing him when sick. NOTHING
   Total NOTHING

How do you think Ali felt? Did he still want to take the three pounds? He learned a very important lesson that day and promised to do helpful things for his mother without expecting payment. He wanted to be helpful in return for all the love he had received.

We should do the same. Remember, too, that God wants people everywhere to be kind and helpful and loving towards other people because *He first loved us*.

Song choices
'He gave me eyes so I could see' (*Junior Praise* 74, *Come and Praise* 18)
'I will make you fishers of men' (*Junior Praise* 123)

Prayer
Loving Heavenly Father, you have shown your love for us in so many ways. Help us to show our love for you by being loving and kind and helpful to our parents and to our friends.
Amen

Extensions/Cross-curricular links
- Younger children could do a topic on people who help us.
- Older children could look at work and try to cost up the true value of different types of job.

20 APRIL FOOLS

8-10 mins

Aim
To show that we are wise when we follow the teaching of Jesus; (to be done on April Fools' Day only!)

Preparation
No preparation is required

When particularly to use
April Fool's Day

Age focus
General

Who can tell me what date it is today?
(*Answer: April 1st*)

What is special about April *1st*?
(*Answer: It is April Fools Day.*)

Today is the day when people like to play tricks on their friends. Have any of you played tricks on your friends? What did you do? You might say to the teacher: 'Please Miss/Sir, your shoe lace is undone!' If I reply 'It can't be because I don't have any shoelaces!' then your trick hasn't worked. You will have to be a little more original! For example, 'Please Miss/Sir, a mouse just ran under your table' or 'Please Miss/Sir, did you know you've got wet paint on the back of your jumper'. If I then say 'Dear me how did I manage that' you would all be able to say 'APRIL FOOL!'.

No one likes to be made to look foolish, but today it doesn't matter provided it is just good harmless fun. But be careful. If it is after twelve noon and you try to play an April Fool trick, everyone will be able to tease *you* and say: 'April Noddy's past and gone, You're the fool for thinking on.'

Remember that April Fools Day is only a game. I hope that at school you will always try to be sensible and not play the fool. You will learn much more and enjoy your work better if you do.

Jesus said that some people are foolish. They are the ones who do not believe what he tells them and do not do what he says. But people who do listen to Jesus' words and do what he tells them, these people, said Jesus, are wise. (*See Matthew Chapter 7 v 24 to 27, and Assembly 1.*)

Prayer
Thank you for our friends, Lord, and for the fun we have together. Thank you, too, that you are a friend to each one of us. Help us to be wise, to listen to your words and to do what you want us to do. Amen

Song choices
(*For older children*) 'The King of love my Shepherd is' (*Junior Praise* 241, *Come and Praise* 54)
(*For younger children*) 'The wise man built his house upon the rock' (*Junior Praise* 252)
'The wise may bring their learning' (*Come and Praise* 64)

Extensions/Curriculum links
• Researching the origins of April Fools' Day and other such customs.
• Creative writing about April Fools' Day pranks.

21 HOT CROSS BUNS — 6-8 mins

Theme
The meaning of Easter

Preparation
Obtain a hot cross bun!

When particularly to use
Near Easter

Age focus
General/Infant

Can anyone tell me what this is? (*Show bun.*) It is a special type of bun which may be bought in bakeries at Easter time. It is a hot cross bun.

There is a very old song which children used to sing while they skipped in the street. This is how it goes:
> Hot cross buns, hot cross buns,
> One a penny, two a penny,
> Hot cross buns.
> If you have no daughters, give them to your sons
> One a penny, two a penny,
> Hot cross buns.

How many of you know that song? (*If there are enough children who know it, it could be sung together.*)

Have you ever wondered why they are called hot cross buns? The shape of the cross on top of the bun is intended to remind us that Jesus died upon a cross on Good Friday. When you eat your hot cross buns on Good Friday, remember that Jesus loves you. Let's say thank you to him.

Prayer
Lord Jesus we thank you that you have shown your love for us as you went to the cross at Easter time. Help us to show how grateful we are by being loving and kind to each other. Amen

Song choices
'There is a green hill far away' (*Junior Praise* 245)
'Jesus' love is very wonderful' (*Junior Praise* 139)
'Jesus Christ is here' Note verse 3. (*Come and Praise* 26)

Extensions/Cross-curricular links
- Investigating Easter customs.
- Cookery: making simple Easter food.

22 EASTER EGGS — 6-8 mins — RS11

Theme
The meaning of Easter - New Life

Preparation
You need an OHT or copymaster of Resource Sheet 11; an Easter egg

When particularly to use
Near Easter

Age focus
General/Infant

We begin today by looking at some pictures of baby animals. (*Show the OHT of baby animals.*)

    What do you call a baby dog?
    What do you call a baby cat?
    What do you call a baby cow?
    What do you call a baby sheep?
    What do you call a baby horse?
    What do you call a baby hen?
    What do you call a baby goose?
    What do you call a baby duck?
    What do you call a baby swan?

A hen, a goose, a duck and a swan all have something in common. Can you guess what it is? They are all birds and they all hatch from eggs.

Have you ever been to a zoo? What baby animals did you see there?

Spring is a lovely time of the year when lots of baby animals are born. After the cold dreary winter days everything seems to be coming back to life again. This is why we give eggs like this (*show eggs*) to our friends at Easter time. They remind us of baby chicks at a time when nature is waking up and coming to life once more.

We remember someone very special at Easter time. We remember to thank God for Jesus, who came to life again on Easter Sunday.

Reading for older children
Mark Chapter 16 v 1 to 7

Song choices
'Morning has broken' (*Come and Praise* 1, *Junior Praise* 166)
'God's not dead, He is alive' (*Junior Praise* 60)

Prayer
Heavenly Father, we thank you for the beauty of the world you have made, for the buds beginning to form on the trees, for the colourful Spring flowers, for the birds that sing merrily, for the baby animals which are being born. As the countryside comes to life once more we thank you that Jesus came to life again at Easter time; that he is alive today and wants to be our Friend, to help and to guide us in all we do. Amen

Extensions/Curriculum links
- Science work on life cycles and reproduction.
- Younger children can write and make baby animals books, perhaps using pictures from the Resource Sheet.

23 PASS IT ON!

12-15 mins

Theme
Passing on good news

Preparation
You will need to prepare a large sheet of paper with the following message written on it (or any other message that you would like to use): 'Terry has just got a new pet dog named Tinker. It has one white paw and three black paws and a left ear which flops down over its eye. Pass it on!'

When particularly to use
Ascension Day

Age focus
General

Today we are going to play a game called 'Pass it on!'. I will tell the first person some news and finish by saying 'pass it on'. That person will then tell the news to the person next to them until the news has been passed all round the class. Of course you will have to speak very quietly so that only the person you are speaking to will be able to hear. (*If doing a whole school assembly, just select one row or group.*)

I am going to tell (*child's name*) my piece of news.

(*In a quiet whisper*) Terry has just got a new pet dog named Tinker. It has one white paw and three black paws and a left ear which flops down over its eye. Pass it on!

(*When the message has been passed all round the class ask the last person who receives it to tell it aloud to the whole class. Then either:*)

Somewhere along the line my piece of news got changed. Either someone didn't speak clearly or someone didn't listen properly. This is what I said. (*Show and read words on the sheet.*)

(*or*)
That message finished up remarkably like the one I gave to (*child's name*) in the first place. It shows you are all very good listeners.

There is another piece of very good news which Jesus says we should pass on to as many people as possible. It is the good news that God loved the world so much that he sent his Son, Jesus to be our Saviour. Before Jesus returned to his Heavenly Father he told his disciples to go into all the world to tell every person this good news. Pass it on! (*See Mark Chapter 16 v 15.*)

Prayer
Show us, good Lord, how we can pass on the good news of your love to other people, by the words that we say and the deeds that we do, for in so doing we are helping to make the world a happier place. Amen

Song choices
'Go tell it on the mountain' (*Junior Praise* 65, *Come and Praise* 24)
'We've a story to tell.' (*Junior Praise* 272)

Extensions/Curriculum links
- Speaking and listening work on oral messages.
- Write good news stories about Jesus in RE.

24 WIND
10-12 mins RS12

Theme
To show that the world God has made is a very wonderful place, and that God gives us the strength we need

Preparation
None but you might like to use Resource Sheet 12 as an OHT or copymaster; you might also like to have a blank OHT to record children's thoughts about the wind.

When particularly to use
Whitsuntide, on a windy day

Age focus
General

Put up your hands if you have ever seen the wind.

Well, that's strange. I haven't! Have you ever seen what the wind has done?
(*Encourage the children to make comments and record them on a blank OHT.*) eg
'I saw the wind blowing the leaves off the trees.' 'I saw the wind blowing the dry sand off the beach.' 'I saw the wind blowing the sails of the boats on the lake.' 'I saw the wind turning the sails of the windmill.' 'I saw the wind turning an umbrella inside out.'

(*Optional*) Here are some pictures which I found of the wind at work. (*Show OHT.*)

You were quite right in what you saw. You saw what the wind was doing but you could not actually see the wind itself. You can feel it, sometimes nearly blowing you over but you can't actually see it.

It's a good job we have the wind, for some of the reasons you have already given me. The wind is also very important because it brings along different kinds of weather. It is the wind which blows in the warm weather and again, the wind makes it nice and fresh when we become too hot. It is the wind which brings along the clouds which give us the rain, to water plants and crops and provide us with water to drink.

Sometimes we forget to thank God for the wonderful things he gives us, so this morning we will give him our thanks for different kinds of weather and especially for wind.

The psalm we are going to hear today reminds us that we should always remember to thank God for the wonderful world he has made.

Reading
Psalm 100 (*Good News Bible*)

Song choices
'All things bright and beautiful' (*Junior Praise* 6, *Come and Praise*)
'For the beauty of the earth' (*Come and Praise* 11, *Junior Praise* 48)
'Who put the colours in the rainbow' (*Junior Praise* 288, *Come and Praise* 12)

Prayer
Father God, we thank you for making this wonderful world and for giving us the different kinds of weather we need. We thank you for refreshing wind and rain and also for warmth and sunshine. Amen

For older children
The Christian Church will soon be celebrating Whitsuntide. This festival is one where we remember that Jesus promised his Spirit, his power and strength to his followers. Jesus said that this is rather like the wind, although you can't see it you know it is there. Although we can't see God's power we can see the difference it makes in our lives. (*See John Chapter 3 v 9.*)

Extensions/curriculum links
- Technology projects making wind-powered machines.
- Ways of recording wind for weather records.

25 SILHOUETTES

6-8 mins   **RS13**

Theme
To show that things will become clearer as we get older. (This assembly is particularly suitable for transfer from Junior to Secondary School.)

Preparation
You need Resource Sheet 13 as an OHT or copymaster. You may also like to get children in a class to create silhouettes of each other. This could be done by rigging up a reading lamp, horizontal to the person's head who is standing side on to a sheet of paper fixed to the wall. Trace round the outline of the shadow cast and paint in with black paint.

When particularly to use
End of the school year

Age focus
General/Upper Junior

Who can tell me, what is a silhouette?

(*Answer*) It is the outline only, of a person or thing usually done in solid black against a white background.

See if you can identify these objects from their silhouettes. (*Show OHT of copymaster.*) And do you recognise these people? (*If using the silhouettes of people as well.*)

It would have been much easier to tell what they were if, instead of a black shadow, we could also see all the details.

In your time in Primary school you have been given a very good broad outline of many subjects but not in any great detail. This should have whetted your appetite for more information. When you get to Secondary school you will be able to continue your studies in far greater detail. You will discover that the older you get the clearer things will become but you will never be in a situation where you will be able to say, 'I know it all!'

This reading from the Bible tells us that at present we may only have a vague outline of what God is like but that one day we will be able to see clearly.

Reading
1 Corinthians Chapter 13 (*Good News Bible*)

Prayer
Thank you, God, for this school, for the lessons we have learned and for the friends we have made. May we never forget them. Help us to learn more and more as we go to our new schools but help us also to learn of your ways and to see more clearly how we might serve you. Amen

Song choices
'Father I place into your hands' (*Junior Praise* 42)
'One more step along the world I go' (*Junior Praise* 188, *Come and Praise* 47)
'Heavenly Father may Thy blessing' (*Come and Praise* 62)

Extensions/Curriculum links
- Children can create their own silhouettes as part of science work on light sources and the formation of shadows.

26 CRABS 6-8 mins RS14

Aim
To show that we should put into practice the good advice we receive.

Preparation
None is required, but you may like to show Resource Sheet 14 as an OHT or copymaster.

When particularly to use
End of the school year

Age focus
General

You will soon be enjoying your summer holidays. Maybe you will have the chance of going to the seaside. What sort of things do you like doing at the seaside? I used to enjoy searching amongst the rocks, catching crabs and putting them in a bucket of water.

Have you ever caught a crab?
How may legs do crabs have? (*Ten, the first pair being like pincers.*)
How does a crab walk? (*Sideways*)
Here is a picture of one. (*Show OHT.*)

Here is a children's story about a group of crabs who always used to meet together on a Sunday afternoon. I suppose you could call it a Crabs' Sunday School! They all used to listen intently to their leader telling them what they should do and how to behave. One Sunday afternoon their 'teacher' said, 'Have you noticed that all the other creatures walk in a forwards direction, yet we crabs have to walk sideways? I'm going to teach you how to use your legs to walk forwards like everyone else.'

So all the crabs practised very hard that afternoon until they could walk forwards. Next Sunday the leader arrived early to wait for all the other crabs to come. When they did start to arrive he was dismayed to see that they were all walking sideways again. They had all forgotten what they had been taught.

I hope we human beings don't have the same problem. What use is it to be given good advice in our assemblies and lessons if we do not then remember it and try hard to practise it day by day?

When you return to school after the holiday you will probably be in a different year group. I hope you will remember all you have been taught this year. Have a good holiday.

Prayer
Thank you Lord for the lessons we have learned during the year and for the good advice we have been given. Help us to remember this and to try to live day by day as you would have us live. Help us to enjoy our holiday, keep us safe and grant that we shall return refreshed and looking forward to a new school year. Amen

Song choices
'One more step along the world I go' (*Junior Praise* 188, *Come and Praise* 47)
'Heavenly Father may Thy blessing' (*Come and Praise* 62)

Extensions/Curriculum links
- Children can study crabs and other sea creatures as part of science work on life processes and living things.
- Younger children can be given the resource sheet to carry out illustrated and annotated factual writing about crabs.

27 CHINESE NEW YEAR — 6-8 mins — RS15

Aim
To show that people are different the world over

Preparation
You need Resource Sheet 15, preferably as an OHT, showing the Chinese years.

When particularly to use
Chinese New year

Age focus
General

Are you an ox or a snake or a dragon or maybe even a monkey?

You will no doubt reply that you are none of these because you are a girl or a boy. But if you lived in China you would also be linked with the name of one of twelve animals as well as having the name your parents gave you, because the Chinese people give each new year the name of a different animal. This is how it all came about.

Chinese legend
Long ago, twelve animals had an argument about the name they would each give to the new year. Each animal thought that the year should be called after its own name. The best way to sort it out, they decided, would be to have a race across a river. From the start the ox took the lead and looked certain to win but he didn't notice that a small rat had climbed on to his back.

Just as the ox neared the far bank the rat jumped off and landed first. The rat won the race and the finishing order was: Rat, Ox, Tiger, Rabbit, Snake, Horse, Sheep, Monkey, Chicken, Dog, Pig.

All agreed that the first year would be called 'The year of the Rat', the second would be called 'The year of the Ox', the third would be called 'The year of the Tiger' and so on.

If you study this chart (*show OHT*) and look up the year you were born you will then know which Chinese year it was and which animal you are.

Chinese people believe that newly born babies are given some of the qualities of the animal of their year. Perhaps you wouldn't mind having the qualities of a dog, for a dog is known for its faithfulness, its affection and as a protector. But how would you like to be a pig? You no doubt think of a pig wallowing in mud but it is, in fact, a very clean animal, renowned for its persistence. These are good qualities to have.

As the Chinese have found out we all have different qualities, different features, different abilities. People are different the world over.

Prayer
Thank you God for the lessons we can learn from people in other parts of the world. Thank you that we are all different. Help us to remember that you made us all and, as your children, we should try to understand and appreciate one another. Amen

Song choices
'He's got the whole world in his hands' (*Junior Praise* 78, *Come and Praise* 190)
'God knows me' (Please note verse 4.) (*Come and Praise* 15)

Extensions/Curriculum links
- Produce charts showing what year children in the class/school were born in; a whole class display could be made.
- Study Chinese customs in more depth as part of work on distant places.

28 GURU NANAK'S CARPET — 6-8 mins

Aim
To show that we should learn to care for all God's creatures

Age focus
General

Preparation
Prepare large cards with the names 'Guru Nanak' and 'Sikh' written on them.

Guru Nanak is the name of a religious teacher who founded the Sikh religion in India in the 15th century. This is how his name is written, and this is the name of the religion he founded. (*Show name cards.*) The name 'Guru' means 'teacher'.

Story
Here is a sacred Sikh story about Guru Nanak and the carpet.

People in India liked to show how much they loved and respected Guru Nanak by giving him presents. Young and old, rich and poor alike would bring their gifts for their very special teacher. But Nanak did not keep the gifts himself. Instead he used them to help poorer people who were not as fortunate.

One day a carpet weaver decided he would like to make a very special gift for the Guru, the best carpet he had ever made. The carpet took months to make and when it was finished the weaver thought to himself 'the Guru will be very pleased to sit on my lovely carpet'.

So he set off to visit the Guru. When he unrolled his beautiful carpet for Nanak to see he said, 'Honour me, my master, by sitting on my carpet.'

Instead Guru said, 'Nature's carpet - the grass - is good enough for me. Please put the carpet to good use for me. See that dog over there with puppies dying of cold and hunger, put the carpet over them and give them food and milk. It would make me happy to save them from suffering.'

So the weaver did as he was commanded and in so doing made Guru Nanak happy and saved the lives of the animals. He himself realised what a good deed he had done.

Guru Nanak had a love and concern for all God's creatures. Christian people, too, are taught in the Bible to care for all God's creatures.

Reading
(*This is part of Psalm 8.*) 'You have made man only a little lower than the angels... you have put him in charge of everything you made; everything is put under his authority; all sheep and oxen, and wild animals too, the birds and fish, and all the life in the sea.'

Prayer
(*From the words of Guru Nanak.*) O God, may I serve you in my childhood and think of you in my youth and in my old age. Amen

Song choices
'Stand up, clap hands, shout thank you Lord' (*Junior Praise* 225)
'All the animals' (*Come and Praise* 80)

Extensions/Curriculum links
- Find out more about the Sikh religion.

29 I CAN'T

8-10 mins

Aim
To show that God is able to help us to do the things he wants us to do

Age focus
General

Preparation
Prepare large cards with the names 'Mohammed' and 'Moses' written on them.

Do you ever say 'I can't do that !'? You will be surprised just what you can do if you really put your mind to it.

We have two stories, from different religions, of people who both said 'I can't' and then found that God was able to use them in a very special way. The first story is from the Islamic faith and is about the founder of that religion, Mohammed.

How Mohammed learnt to read
Mohammed was an orphan boy who lived first with his grandfather and then with an uncle who both loved and cared for him. Unfortunately they were not able to teach him to read. Though Mohammed lived among people who worshipped many idols - gods made out of wood or stone - he worshipped one great God. Little did he realise what a great part he would play in telling others of his faith.

When Mohammed was forty years of age, while he was praying, the Angel Gabriel came to him in a vision with a book in the form of a scroll and said 'Read!'

'I cannot read,' replied Mohammed who was afraid. Then Gabriel put his arms around him, holding him tightly. 'Read!' said Gabriel once more. 'I cannot read,' said Mohammed. A third time the angel told him to read and a third time Mohammed insisted that he was not able to read.

'Read in the name of the Lord who createth man....thy Lord is most generous, who teaches man the use of the pen and teaches him what he did not know before.' Mohammed knew he would never forget those words, from that moment on he could read and write.

He had been given a power of language which he was able to use to teach the will of God to the people of Islam.

Gabriel's last words were, 'Mohammed, you are the messenger of Allah (God)!' And so the Islamic religion began.

How Moses freed the Israelites
Our second story is about a young man named Moses who became one of the forefathers of the Jewish religion.

One day as Moses was looking after the sheep which belonged to his father-in-law Jethro, an angel appeared to him in the flames of a bush which was on fire. He then heard God's voice calling him, 'Moses, Moses! I want you to go to Egypt and speak to Pharaoh (the king). Tell him to let God's people go free.' The Israelites had been kept as prisoners in Egypt for many years.

'But I'm not the person for the job,' said Moses, 'I can't do that!'. Even though God promised to be with Moses, to help him, Moses kept on making excuse after excuse. 'Pharaoh won't listen to me,' said Moses. 'I am not a good speaker - I never have been.'

But the Lord God insisted. 'Now do as I say for I will help you to speak well and will tell you what to say.'

Eventually Moses obeyed, taking his brother Aaron with him for support and in time was able to lead the Israelites out of Egypt into the land which God had promised them would be theirs.

Both these great men at first said, 'I can't do that' but then found that when they obeyed God's command they were given the strength they needed.

Prayer
Father God help us always to try to do your will. When we fear that things may be very difficult, give to us your strength we pray and show us the things we can do. Amen

Song choices
'Father I place into your hands' (*Junior Praise* 2) 'You shall go out with joy' (*Come and Praise 98*)

Extensions/Curriculum links
- Find out more about Mohammed and Islam.
- Study the life of Moses in RE.

30 DRAGON BOATS — 10-12 mins — RS16

Aim
To give the children an insight into another culture

Preparation
You need Resource Sheet 16 as an OHT; you need the word 'festival' written on a large card. A blank OHT could also be used to collect children's suggestions.

When particularly to use
June

Age focus
General

Introduction
Which is the most important day of the year for you? (*Invite suggestions from the children.*)

A person's birthday is usually the most important day for them. What sort of things do you do on your birthday in order to make it special? (*Invite suggestions from the children.*)

A birthday is like a festival - it is a special celebration - when we have fun and games and lots of nice things to eat. We have a feast and that is why it is called a 'festival'. Here is the word 'festival'. (*Show card.*)

Can you think of any other festivals we celebrate in this country during the year?

A list such as the following may be compiled on the OHT: New Year; Shrove Tuesday (Pancake Day); Easter; May Day; Harvest; Hallo'een; Bonfire Night; Christmas.

These are festivals for everyone to enjoy. In other countries people have different festivals.

Dragon boats
I want to tell you today about a festival held in China every June. It is called dragon boat racing. It all started in China over 2000 years ago. A Chinese legend tells of a warrior who became a poet, whose name was Ch'u Yuen. He was a loyal subject of the Emperor but was very concerned about the corruption and evil ways of the government of his day.

In order to make his protest about this, Ch'u Yuen went out in a boat on the Mi Lo river and drowned himself. When the people heard of this tragedy they took to the river in their boats to search for his body. They beat drums in the boats and hit the water with their paddles to frighten away evil spirits and they threw rice dumplings into the water so that fish would not harm Ch'u Yuen's body.

Every year, since then, a dragon boat festival is held on the 5th day of the 5th moon (that is June on our calendar) to remember the death of Ch'u Yuen. It has become such an important sporting event in China that it is as important as the London Marathon or the Wembley Cup Final are in England.

The boats are 40 feet long and are paddled by a team of 16 to 20 people sitting in twos. At the front of each boat is a Chinese emblem of a dragon's head, ornately carved and painted and bristling with sharp leaves of grass. Behind this head sits the drummer, beating loudly to get the last ounce of energy from the crew.

The sport is taken so seriously in China that there are special dragon boat schools. Professional crew members are paid by the government to train many hours every day. International events are held all over the world with British teams competing.

Festivals give us the opportunity to have lots of fun and make merry but they should also be a time when we look back to some important event or some renowned person and give thanks.

Prayer
We give you thanks, O God, for the special days in our lives, for the happiness these festivals bring. Help us to remember the good people who did so much to help others less fortunate than themselves and often risked their own lives in so doing. As we look to the future help us to promise to serve you and our neighbours to the very best of our ability. Amen

Song choices
'You shall go out with joy' (*Come and Praise* 98)
'Kum ba yah' (*Junior Praise* 149, *Come and Praise* 68)
'Let us with a gladsome mind' (*Junior Praise* 154, *Come and Praise* 8)
'When a knight won his spurs' (*Come and Praise* 50)

Extensions/Curriculum links
- Design a dragon boat or make a scale model.
- Research customs and festivals round the world as part of a major topic.
- Study Chinese customs in more depth as part of work on distant places.
- Give children a copy of the Resource Sheet and ask them to write an exciting account of a dragon boat race.

31 FESTIVALS OF LIGHT   6-8 mins

Theme
We all need light.

Preparation
You need as many different light sources as you can obtain e.g. a light bulb, a torch, a candle in holder with matches, an oil lamp, a gas camping lamp, car lights etc. A blank OHT will also be useful to write children's suggestions on.

When particularly to use
This is the first in a series of five assembly themes which show how people of different faiths give thanks for light. The series can be treated as a unit or used individually at appropriate times of the year.

Age focus
General

We all need light to live by. How many things can you think of which give light?

(*Encourage the children to suggest the following. You can write the suggestions on a blank OHT if you like:*)
- electric light bulbs (*a child could be asked to demonstrate by switching on the room lights*)
- torches (*demonstrate and explain how the battery is the source of power*)
- candles, matches (*the candle could be placed in a candlestick and then lit by you. Ensure that you explain the dangers.*)
- oil lamps (*again carefully demonstrate, stressing the dangers.*)
- fireworks
- gas lamps
- car lights

All these lights help us to see in the dark. They are all made by people for this purpose. Can you think of anything which is not 'man-made' which gives light? (*Hopefully children will list the sun, moon, stars, lightening, glow worms even!*)

What is the most important light source of all? The sun of course. Without sunshine there could not be any life - it would be far too cold. Without sunshine plants could not grow - there would be no harvest.

Thousand of years ago people who knew no better used to worship the sun thinking that it was some sort of god which provided warmth, light and life. Today, people all over the world still realise how important the sun is.

In winter time the hours of daylight are much shorter and the weather colder. Everyone looks forward to the coming of spring - to warmer days when there is more light and sunshine.

So it is that people of many different faiths, in many different countries celebrate the return of the light. Special parties or festivals are held to give thanks for light. We shall learn about some of these during this week, but today we shall simply thank God for the light.

Prayer
Dear God, we thank you that when you made the universe, the world in which we live, you gave us light. Thank you God for the sun which provides us with light, warmth and life itself. Amen

Song
'For the beauty of the earth' (*Junior Praise* 48, *Come and Praise* 11)

Extensions/Curriculum links
- Science work on light sources.

32 CHINESE LIGHTS — 6-8 mins — RS17

Theme
The Chinese festival of light

Time
6-8 mins (plus the time for the procession)

Preparation
None but the assembly will have much more significance if it is part of a larger class project in which children have already made artefacts that relate to the festival: individual paper lanterns and a large Chinese dragon as described in the assembly. You can use Resource Sheet 17 as an OHT instead.

When particularly to use
Spring

Age focus
General

In the great country of China, the people welcome the coming of spring and return of lighter, warmer days with a lantern festival. Children make brightly coloured lanterns out of silk, glass, stalks of wheat and paper. They are painted with pictures of old Chinese stories. The lanterns are then hung from the tops of poles. A huge dragon is made and carried by several people as they process through the streets. Here is a picture of a Chinese dragon. (*Show OHT.*) Special foods are prepared for all the family to eat.

(*Optional*) Let us pretend that we are in China as we now join in a festival of light. (*Lead the children along a chosen route using the dragon and lanterns made in craft lessons.*)

Prayer
We praise you and thank you, O God, for your promise of lighter, warmer days, that spring always follows winter. Help us always to be grateful for your goodness to us. Amen

Song choices
'Stand up, clap hands, shout thank you' (*Junior Praise* 225)
'Thank you Lord' (*Come and Praise* 32)

Extensions/Curriculum links
- Art and Craft lessons making Chinese artefacts.
- Use Resource Sheet 17 for creative writing.

33 DIWALI

6-8 mins

Theme
How Hindus and Sikhs celebrate light

Preparation
None but the assembly would be greatly enriched by being linked into a class project on Diwali.

When particularly to use
Autumn

Age focus
General

Followers of the Hindu and Sikh faiths have their own festival of lights which they call Diwali. This word means 'a cluster of lights'.

They place lamps outside their homes each year in October or November for a special reason. They are remembering something which happened many hundreds of years ago when similar lamps were lit to guide their favourite Prince - Rama and his wife Sita home to safety after a battle. These lamps were needed to light up the darkness.

Other festivals of light are held by Hindus and Sikhs in honour of their ancestors who founded their faith. These people they call Gurus or teachers. Many of these Gurus were punished and put in prison because of their beliefs. Sikh people celebrate Diwali to commemorate the birthday of their Guru named Nanak and another one named Hargobind.

Guru Hargobind arranged for the release of some Hindu princes from prison. When he returned to Amritsar in 1620 the Sikhs lit up the Golden Temple in his honour.

Hindus celebrate Diwali in honour of their Goddess Lakshmi, who they believe will bring wealth and prosperity and will visit the homes which are well prepared, carefully cleaned and decorated. Extra oil lamps are brought out and new clothes worn for this Hindu festival which is held at the end of the old year and the beginning of the new.

So for both Hindus and Sikhs, for different reasons, Diwali is a time for rejoicing with lights, fireworks, sweets and a huge party.

Today we are going to use a Hindu prayer:
>O God, you are the giver of life,
>The healer of pains and sorrows,
>The giver of happiness.
>O Creator of the Universe,
>Send us your purifying light
>And lead our thoughts in your ways.
>Amen

Song
'He gave me eyes so I could see' (*Junior Praise* 74, *Come and Praise* 18)

Extensions/Curriculum links
- A class project in RE on Diwali.

34 HANUKKAH

6-8 mins — **RS18**

Theme
Hanukkah, the Jewish festival of light

Preparation
You need Resource Sheet 18 as an OHT or copymaster. This assembly again would be enriched by outside class work on Hanukkah.

When particularly to use
December

Age focus
General

The Jewish people also have a special festival of light which is held at the same time as the Christian festival of Christmas. Hanukkah means dedication. Over two thousand years ago there was bitter fighting between the Jews and their neighbours the Syrians. The Jew's holiest temple had been taken over by the Syrians who had put out all the lights. No longer were the Jewish people allowed to worship God in their temple.

Eventually, the Jewish people were delivered from their enemies. They got their temple back and immediately lit the temple lamp. But there was only enough oil to keep the lamp burning for one night. Miraculously the lamp continued to burn, lighting up the temple for eight days.

The festival Hanukkah is the way the Jews give thanks to God for enabling the light to return to their temple. During this festival, in Jewish homes, you will see a special candle holder called a Hanukkah Menorah which holds eight candles and a ninth in the centre for lighting all the others. On the first night of Hanukkah the first candle is lit. Each night after that, one more candle is lit until on the last night all eight are alight.

Here is a picture of a Menorah. This is a traditional Jewish seven branched candlestick, similar to the one with nine candleholders used in the festival of Hanukkah. (*Show OHT.*)

Reading
Listen now to part of a psalm of David which the Jewish people love to read.
(*Read Psalm 27 v 1-4.*)

Prayer
Father in Heaven, as the Jewish people give you thanks for the light which returned to their temple so we give you our thanks for your special light which comes into our lives at Christmas time. Help us to so live our lives that we may be like lamps which help to bring light and happiness to other people. Amen

Song
'Give me oil in my lamp' (*Junior Praise* 50, *Come and Praise* 43)

Extensions/Curriculum links
- Class project on Hanukkah.
- Use the resource sheet as part of a wall display.

35 CHRISTMAS LIGHT — 6-8 mins

Theme
Advent: the Christian festival of light

Preparation
You need a Christmas tree decorated with lights but not switched on.

When particularly to use
Advent

Age focus
General

Christian people have their own festival of light. It lasts for four weeks during the period we call Advent, leading up to Christmas day. During this time we think of how God's light has come into the world showing us how we should live. In Christian churches throughout the world, on the four Sundays before Christmas, Advent candles are lit.

In homes throughout the land Christmas trees are put on display and are lit up with special 'fairy' lights. In the olden days, before homes had electricity, candles were fitted to the Christmas trees but when they were lit the naked flames were very dangerous and sometimes the trees would catch fire. Today we are much more fortunate, we can put electric lights on our trees in perfect safety. But why do we do this? Why do we light Advent candles in church? It is not just that we are looking forward to the return of lighter, warmer days in spring but because at Christmas we remember that God sent Jesus to be our Saviour and that Jesus said that he was the Light of the world. He would show us the way to come to God our Father. Christmas tree lights remind us of Jesus the Light of the World and tell us that at Christmas time God's light truly comes into the world.

We shall now light up our Christmas tree. (*Switch on light*.)

Reading
John Chapter l. v l - 5 and 9 - 12

Prayer
We thank you Heavenly Father that at Christmas time you sent your son Jesus to be born at Bethlehem. Thank you Jesus that you are the true light which has come into the world. We ask you to be with us always, showing us how our lives might best please you. Bless us Heavenly Father this Christmas time, bless our homes and those who care for us and bless all who seek to serve you throughout the world. Amen

Song choices
'As with gladness' This is a carol about the Light of the World. (*Junior Praise* 9)
'Colours of day' (*Come and Praise* 55)

Extensions/Curriculum links
- Make class advent calendars, with every window a different kind of light.

36 THE HOKEY COKEY — 10-15 mins

Aim
To encourage a full commitment to school work and to God

Age focus
General

Preparation
If would be helpful, but not essential, to find a recording of the 'Hokey Cokey'. You may also find it useful to have the words available on an OHT. It is suggested that a small group of children from one class learn to do the dance prior to the assembly.

How many of you know how to do the Hokey Cokey? For the benefit of those who don't, I'll teach it to you. (*Read the words and demonstrate! - or get your trained 'team' to do it!*)

> You put your left arm in, your left arm out,
> In out, in out, shake it all about.
> You do the Hokey Cokey and you turn around,
> That's what it's all about.

(*Repeat the above with right arm, then left leg, right leg and finally - you put your whole self in, etc.*)

Some children from class have been practising the dance and they are now going to show you how to do it. (*Children demonstrate.*)

(*At the conclusion*)
The last verse was very hectic, wasn't it? One moment they had put their whole selves in, the next they had taken their whole selves out! Wouldn't it be a shambles if that is how we tried to do our school work? If one day we put our whole effort into our lessons and then the next we took it out again because we didn't listen very carefully or didn't try very hard. Let us try to put our whole selves into our school work all the time.

(*For older pupils*)
Jesus, too, wants his followers to be wholehearted and is saddened if, after beginning to follow his teaching - putting our whole selves in, we forget after a while about him and take ourselves out again.

Reading
Luke Chapter 9 v 61 & 62
Here is an explanation of this passage:
The farmer had begun to plough his field and instead of keeping looking straight ahead, he turned round and as a result made a complete mess of his ploughing. Jesus wants us to look to him as our example and to follow his ways. As in the dance, the Hokey Cokey, we must put our whole selves in, but then we must keep ourselves in and not allow ourselves to be distracted from our intention to follow Jesus.

Prayer
Help us Lord, always to try hard with our work at school but also to keep on serving you and following in your ways. Amen

Song choices
'One more step along the world I go' (*Junior Praise* 188, *Come and Praise* 47)
'Father lead me day by day' (*Junior Praise* 43)

Extensions/Curriculum links
- Other types of dance which can be performed.

37 THE TALKING BOOK 10-12 mins

Aim
To show that God can speak to us through his book.

Age focus
General

Preparation
You need a 'noisy book', e.g. *Fireman Sam,* 'the Bonefire Party' Heinemann ISBN 0-434-97816-7, or any other children's book with electronic sounds; a Bible

---

I'm going to read you a story today from my 'Noisy Book'. It is a special kind of book which can actually make sound. Before I read the story see if you can tell what makes the following noises. (*Press each picture in turn - the children should be able to identify the following sounds:- telephone, alarm bell, siren, cat, horn etc.*) The Fireman Sam story is entitled, 'The Bonfire Party'. (*As the story unfolds various sound effects will be created by pressing the appropriate picture.*)

That was a different kind of story, wasn't it? The book I used is like a talking book - it can make sounds!

I have also brought along another talking book. (*Show them the copy of the Bible.*) In a way this is like a talking book because God himself is able to speak to us through the stories in it. In this way he is able to tell us how he wants us to live.

(*For older children*)
Here are some of the things God wants us to know.
- Love God with all your hearts and other people as much as you love yourselves. (*See Luke Chapter 10 v 27.*)
- Be kind to other people and treat them as you would like them to treat you. (*See Matthew Chapter 7 v 12.*)
- God wants us to follow Jesus and try to live like him. (*See Matthew Chapter 4 v 19.*)
- Jesus wants us to know that if we believe in him and put our trust in him we will be safe. (*See Acts Chapter 16 v 31.*)

Prayer
Dear God, we thank you for your book, the Bible. As we listen to its stories or read it for ourselves, help us to know that you are speaking to us showing us how we can live happy lives. Amen

Song choices
'Tell me the stories of Jesus' (*Junior Praise* 228 - selected verses)
'The best book to read is the Bible' (*Junior Praise* 234)
'A still small voice' (*Come and Praise* 96)

Extensions/Curriculum links
- Children can try making their own simple 'noisy book' using a tape recorder.
- Study of the structure and content of the Bible.

38 KEYHOLES

6-8 mins **RS19**

Aim
To encourage Church attendance. (This is an assembly particularly suitable for a Church school.)

Preparation
You need Resource Sheet 19 as an OHT or photocopy sheet.

Age focus
General

Put up your hands if you recognise this shape. (*Show keyhole diagram.*) It is the shape of a keyhole.

Have you ever had a red, sore eye and someone has said to you, 'That is what happens when you look through a keyhole'? (The draught blowing through the keyhole is said to make your eye go red and watery!)

Of course, it isn't a very nice thing to do, to look through a keyhole in order to see what is in the room. But there is a popular television programme called 'Through the Keyhole'. In the programme the camera peeps through a keyhole into someone's house, showing the viewers just what kind of home it is. A group of contestants then have to guess which famous person lives in that house. The presenter of the programme says at the start, 'Let's now take a look through the keyhole' Then when we have all had a good look round, he says 'Well, whose house is this?'

I want you to pretend you are now looking through a keyhole. I will describe the house and then ask you if you know whose house it is.
- This house has lots and lots of seats, probably several hundred of them.
- This house has beautifully coloured windows at the far end.
- This is a very peaceful, happy house.
- This house belongs to the largest family in the world.
- This house should be full every Sunday but, sadly, many people don't go to it.

Can you guess which house I am describing? Yes! God's house - the Church. Christians throughout the world belong to the largest family - the family of God's people. They love to go to Church on Sundays to sing praises to God their Heavenly Father, to hear stories of Jesus and to say their prayers.

(*For older children:*)
Jesus promised that wherever his followers meet together to worship God, he will be with them. (*See Matthew Chapter 18 v 20.*)

Song choices
'Praise him, praise him' (*Junior Praise* 201)
'The King of love' (*Come and Praise* 54 - please note the last line)

Prayer
Help us, Heavenly Father, to show how grateful we are for your love by singing your praises and by remembering to say thank you when we say our prayers. Amen

Extensions/Curriculum links
- Arrange with the vicar to visit your local church and find out about the features of God's house.
- Use the Resource Sheet as a photocopiable stimulus for writing about looking through the keyhole into a magic world.

39 HANDS

10-15 mins

Aim
To encourage the children to make the best use of their talents

Preparation
This is best done as a class assembly. You need to prepare an outline of your own hands and get members of the class also to trace round their hands. You may also like to have a blank OHT or flipchart sheet for recording suggestions.

When particularly to use
Spring

Age focus
General

Everyone's hands are slightly different although they are very similar. I'm going to ask you each in turn to hold up your diagrams and to say one thing that your hands are good at doing. (*You can list these things on an OHT or flipchart if you like.*)

(*Now show diagram of your own hands.*)

Can you guess whose hands these are? Mine of course. They are good at some things. Not so good at others.
e.g. They can play the piano.
   They can't play the guitar.
   They can write on the chalk board.
   They can't type very well.
   They are reasonably good at gardening.
   They have to be good at washing up the dishes.
   They used to be good at playing tennis.
   (*and so on*)

No one can be good at everything, but everyone is good at something. You may be good at art. Your best friend may be better than you at writing stories. We all have different abilities or talents. As we grow up we should try to use these abilities wisely and fully in order to please God and to help each other.

Prayer
Thank you, Heavenly Father, for our hands which we can use in so many different ways. Thank you for giving us the ability to do certain things very well. Help us always to try hard and to do our best. Amen

Song choices
'Two little eyes to look to God' (*Junior Praise* 262)
'He gave me eyes so I could see' (*Junior Praise* 74, *Come and Praise* 18)

Extensions/Curriculum links
• Shape writing on 'Things my hands can do' within hand shapes.
• Work on hands as part of a science project on 'Me'.

40 FOG

8-10 mins

Aim
To show that we should never worry too much when things seem to get difficult.

Preparation
None is required but a blindfold will be useful if you wish to play the game mentioned below for younger children.

When particularly to use
Winter, foggy weather

Age focus
General

What sort of weather do you not like? Why? (*Invite comments such as the following*:)
- Rain - because I can't go out to play with my friends.
- Hail - because the hailstones hurt my face.
- Snow - because it turns to slush and makes my feet wet.
- Wind - because it takes my breath away.
- Ice - because elderly people might slip and hurt themselves.
- Sun - because I get too hot and feel uncomfortable.
- Cold - because it makes my fingers numb.

The weather I hate most is fog. Why do you think this might be? (*Again invite comments, such as the following*:)
- Fog gets on my chest and makes me cough.
- Cars crash in the fog.
- I can't see where I am going in fog.
- I could get lost in fog.

When you cannot see it is very difficult to find your way around.(*Here, a simple game could be played with younger children in which one player is blindfolded and given directions to find his or her way across the room to a particular spot.*)

I think fog is the worst kind of weather, but thankfully as soon as the sun comes out the fog disappears.

Sometimes when we get puzzled and find our work hard or when we don't understand what we are being told, it is like being in a fog because we can't see or understand clearly what we should do.

If ever you are puzzled and it seems as though you are in a 'fog', don't worry, help is at hand. There are lots of people who will help you to understand - your parents and your teacher will do all they can to help. The imaginary fog will quickly clear away.

Prayer
Heavenly father, when things seem to get very difficult, help us so that we will be able to understand clearly what we should do. Thank you for all the people who are able to help us, our teachers, our parents, older brothers and sisters. May we always be willing to listen to good advice and so live our lives the way you want us to do. Amen

Song choices
'When the road is rough' (*Junior Praise* 279)
'Father, lead me day by day' (*Junior Praise* 43)
'Father hear the prayer we offer' (*Come and Praise* 48)

Extension/curriculum links:
- Science project on weather or the five senses.
- Creative writing: fog is a wonderful theme for mystery and adventure writing.

41 ALARMS

6-8 mins

Theme
Telling the difference between right and wrong

Preparation
You need an alarm clock, and, if possible, a smoke alarm; a blank OHT or flipchart sheet may also be useful.

Age focus
General

Can you guess what sort of clock this is? It is an alarm clock. (*Demonstrate.*)

I rely on this clock every morning, to wake me up and warn me that it is time to be getting ready to come to school. The bell with its loud ring is an alarm - a warning. Can you think of any other alarm bells or sirens? (*You can list these on a blank OHT or flipchart.*)

- The school fire alarm (*Describe this, and if possible get a teacher to demonstrate, and explain again what the children should do if ever it was to go off.*) Having this alarm means that we are quite safe at school.
- Smoke alarm (*show one if you have one.*) It is very important that every home should have one of these. At the first sign of smoke the alarm sounds so that we have good time to get out of the house.
- Police car siren Police cars often have to travel very quickly to the scene of some trouble. The shrill sound of the siren warns other car drivers to keep well clear.
- Ambulance siren It is very important for ambulances to travel fast as they get sick people to hospital. The siren warns everyone to keep clear and not to slow them down.
- It is a good idea to have a loud burglar alarm in your home which would frighten away anyone who tries to break in.

There is just one more alarm I would like to tell you about. We all have one. It tells us whether we are doing right and warns us if we are doing wrong.

If for example we tell a lie or take something which belongs to someone else, something inside us makes us go all hot and bothered, telling us we are doing wrong. This is called our 'conscience'. We do well to listen to what our conscience tell us. It is like an alarm which tells us if we are doing wrong.

If ever our conscience tells us we have behaved badly, then we can make things so much better if we say 'sorry' to the person we have upset and also say sorry to God because he is very sad when people do wrong.

Reading for older children
1 John Chapter 1 v 5 to 10.

Song choices
'Father I place into your hands' (*Junior Praise* 42)
'When the road is deep and rough' (*Junior Praise* 279)
'Heavenly Father may Thy blessing' (*Come and Praise* 62)

Prayer
Thank you, Lord Jesus, that you sometimes speak to us through our consciences. We are sorry that sometimes we do naughty things and we ask you to forgive us and help us to live better lives. Amen

Extensions/Curriculum links
- Constructing alarms with buzzers/ lights and pressure pads.
- Creative writing; 'The day the fire alarm went off…'

42 REMEMBERING

12-15 mins

Aim
To show the importance of good memories and what things we should remember.

Preparation
Time will be required to collect twenty objects on a tray such as a pencil, a rubber, a paper clip, a bus ticket, a ten pence piece, nail clippers, elastic band, diary, teaspoon, tea-bag, piece of chalk, button, tube of toothpaste, paint brush, drawing pin, book mark, a sweet, a purse, a sugar lump, a key. You will need to place these on a tray with a cloth to cover them. It will also be helpful to have a blank OHT or flipchart.

Age focus
General

Today we are going to play a game. Underneath the cloth on this tray are twenty (*reduce the number for younger children*) very familiar things. When I take off the cloth I will give you just one minute to look at the objects on the tray. Then I will cover them up again and I will ask you how many of the objects you are able to remember.

(When the children have had one minute to look at the objects, re-cover the tray and ask the children to put up their hands to tell you, one at a time, which objects they have remembered. When each object is mentioned remove it from the tray and place to one side. When no further answers are forthcoming, the cloth can be removed revealing any objects which were forgotten. With a larger group, larger objects can be used and taken, one at a time, from a box and placed into another box. When the children have seen all the objects they can then be asked which ones they could remember. As each object is named, place it back in its original box. Again, once no further answers are forthcoming, show the children the ones they didn't remember.)

This just goes to show how hard it is to remember things. (*In the event of all the objects being recalled, praise the children for their good memories!*)

Let us now make a list of the things we have to remember each day. (*Pupils may give examples such as the following which can be recorded on an OHT:*)

Remember to:
1. clean our teeth after breakfast.
2. keep our bedrooms tidy.
3. clean our school shoes.
4. say thank you for our breakfast.
5. get to school on time.
6. bring what we need for school.
7. bring back our school library books.
8. close the doors.
9. keep our school tidy.
10. watch our favourite television programme!

I want to mention one other thing we must remember to do. We must always remember to say thank you to God for his love and his help.

Here is a story about ten men who had a disease called leprosy. Jesus was so sorry for them that he healed them. I wonder how many remembered to say 'thank you'. (*Read Luke Chapter 17 v 12 to 17.*) Only one man remembered to say 'thank you'.

Song choices
'Thank you for every new good morning' (*Junior Praise* 230)
'Thank you Lord for this new day' (*Come and Praise* 32)

Prayer
Thank you for the world so sweet,
Thank you for the food we eat,
Thank you for the birds that sing,

Thank you God for everything.
Help us always, Heavenly Father, to remember to say thank you for your love. Amen

Extensions/Curriculum links
- Work in the classroom on developing skills of recall, using mnemonic techniques.
- Writing poems, each verse of which starts 'Thank you'.

43 LUCK

6-8 mins — **RS20**

Aim
To show that God will help us if we trust him

Age focus
General

Preparation
You need a copy of Resource Sheet 20 as an OHT or copymaster and a coin; (for greater dramatic effect when tossing a coin, get the children to make a giant cardboard coin with heads and tails on it.)

Introduction
Do you recognise this?
(*Answer - It is a coin. Its value is ...*).
Whose head is on the front of all British coins?
(*Answer - The Queen's head*)

If I toss the coin in the air it may land with the Queen's head uppermost. We then say that is 'heads'. But if it lands the other way up, we say that is 'tails'. See if you can guess which way it is going to land. How many think it will be heads? How many think it will be tails?

(*Now toss the coin. Do this several times.*)
It was only a matter of luck which way up the coin landed. Some captains of sport's teams have what they think is a lucky coin which they use to toss up before a game starts, believing it will bring good luck to their team. Many teams have lucky mascots.

Here, now, are pictures of two other things which are supposed to bring good luck: a black cat; a horse shoe (*show pictures*).

Here are pictures of two things which are supposed to bring bad luck: a ladder; the number 13 (*show pictures*) Why do you think people don't like walking under ladders?

Some people believe in luck and even trust to luck. But there is a much better way. In all the important things in life we need not just trust to luck - we should trust in the Lord Jesus. Jesus promises to be with us, to help us and to guide us. 'Trust in the Lord with all your heart' - this is so much better than trusting to luck.

Reading
Proverbs Chapter 3 v 5 & 6

Prayer
Heavenly Father you have promised to be with us in all that we do. Whenever we have problems or difficulties help us to put our trust in you. Amen

Song
'God who made the earth.....will care for me' (*Junior Praise* 63, *Come and Praise* 10)

Extensions/Curriculum links
• Research into lucky and unlucky superstitions.
• Creative writing about luck in stories.
Statistical work: does a coin always land heads and tails the same number of times?

44 HORSESHOE NAIL

6-8 mins — **RS20**

Aim
To show that everyone is important

Age focus
General

Preparation
You need a horseshoe, or use the diagram on Resource Sheet 20.

Who can tell me what this is? It is a horseshoe, a curved piece of strong metal which is fitted painlessly to the underneath of the horse's hoof with special nails by a blacksmith. Have any of you ever seen a blacksmith at work? (*Ask for contributions.*) How does the blacksmith fit the shoe? Horseshoes protect the hooves so that the horse will not go lame.

Story

Long ago, when battles were fought on horseback, with swords, spears and bows and arrows, there lived a king who was afraid that his kingdom was about to be attacked by an enemy army. So he sent 'look outs' to the far corners of his kingdom with instructions to watch out for enemy soldiers approaching. If spotted, they should saddle their horses and ride as fast as possible to warn the king of danger.

When the enemy army was spotted one messenger quickly got his horse ready and started out on the long journey to warn the king. But in his haste he didn't notice that one of the nails holding a horseshoe had worked loose. As he rode along the shoe came off and this slowed the horse down so much that the messenger arrived too late. The king and his army were taken by surprise and lost not only the battle but the kingdom itself. If only that little horseshoe nail had not worked loose!

This story is in the form of a poem:
> For want of a nail the shoe was lost.
> For want of a shoe the horse was lost.
> For want of a horse the rider was lost.
> For want of a rider the message was lost.
> For want of a message the battle was lost.
> For want of a battle the kingdom was lost.
> And all for the want of a horseshoe nail.

A little horseshoe nail: what a small unimportant thing you may think! Yet it brought defeat for the king's army.

You may sometimes feel that you, like the horseshoe nail, are small and unimportant when you see what a big school this is. But every person is needed to make the school a happy place. One person could spoil it for everyone else. You are all important.

(For older children)
In the gospel story, Jesus tells us that we are all important to God, who loves us and cares for us. So much does God care for us that he knows how many hairs we have on our heads. (*See Matthew Chapter 10 v 30.*) He loves us so much, each one of us, that he sent Jesus to be our Friend and Saviour.

Song choices

'Jesus loves me this I know' (*Junior Praise* 140)
'Jesus' love is very wonderful' (*Junior Praise* 139)
'Jesus good above all other' (*Come and Praise* 23)

Prayer

Dear God, we thank you for our school, for our friends and our teachers. Help us all to play our part in making it a happy place. Amen

Extensions/Curriculum links

- Research into the work of blacksmiths.
- Science work on the properties of iron as a material.

45 NEW CLOTHES

8-10 mins

Aim
To help the children to think of others and not just themselves.

Age focus
General

Preparation
None is required, but if working with a small group of younger children you may like to tell the story with the aid of a book such as the pop-up version *The Emperor's new Clothes* Grandreams Ltd ISBN 1 85830-108-4.

Introduction
Before you leave home in the morning for school it is a good idea to have a quick glance in the mirror to check that you are properly dressed, that your face is clean and your hair combed and tidy.

Our story today is of an important emperor who just loved to look at himself in the mirror. He spent hours doing this and never thought of anyone but himself.

Story
Once upon a time there lived an Emperor who was full of his own importance. He thought only of himself and his appearance - how grand he looked. All he could think of were clothes and how handsome he was. All the spare rooms and cupboards throughout the palace were filled with the Emperor's fine clothes, shoes and crowns. Whenever he got dressed he would stand for ages admiring himself in the mirror. His reputation spread throughout the kingdom so that all the weavers, tailors and cobblers in the land were kept busy.

One day, two strangers called at the Emperor's palace. They had heard of the Emperor's liking for clothes and thought they may be able to trick him and make a lot of money for themselves. They told the guards, 'We are weavers and we have a very special magical new cloth to show the Emperor.'

The Emperor welcomed them inside and set them to work straight away. The two weavers soon realised that the Emperor was so vain that they would be able to trick him. This was their plan. They asked for a loom and sacks of gold coins so that they could begin to weave this special magical gold cloth.

They told the Emperor it would feel like silk, be as warm as wool, light as air and would have radiant colours, with gold and silver.

When, at last, they said they had finished the cloth they explained, 'Only the truly wise will be able to see it - that is why it is magical!' The Emperor and all his courtiers didn't wish to seem ignorant so they all said the new cloth was indeed beautiful, even though, in fact, there was nothing at all for them to see.

'There is a grand parade in a few weeks time,' the Emperor told the weavers, 'and I want you to make me a complete new outfit with this new cloth, especially for the occasion.'

So the weavers got to work again, and took all the measurements and pretended to make new clothes for the Emperor. They then took all the gold they were offered and fled from the palace and the country. Meanwhile, the servants helped the Emperor to dress in his new invisible outfit, not daring to admit they had all been tricked. He even stood in front of the mirror longer than usual admiring himself. 'My, what a handsome man I am,' he thought.

The day for the grand parade arrived and the townsfolk lined the streets to see the Emperor's new clothes. No one dared to say a word, except one small boy who exclaimed, 'The Emperor isn't wearing any clothes, he's absolutely naked!'

It was then that the crowd began to laugh and laugh, but the Emperor who realised he had been tricked also felt very ashamed. 'In future I will take advice from other people, for they also are important,' he said. 'I must stop thinking too much about myself and more about other people.'

That day, the Emperor learned a very important lesson. We, too, must learn the same lesson - that we are all important but that no-one should feel too important. It is so much better if we all learn to share things and take turns, instead of thinking, 'I am the only one that matters.'

(*For older children*)
Jesus, himself, sets us a very good example to follow. Though he was sent from God, he didn't arrive in the world with a great show of pomp and ceremony but was born in a lowly cattle shed. When he became a man he was humble enough to wash his disciples' feet and he said we must all serve one another.

Reading
John Chapter 13 v 3 to 5 and 12 to 15

Prayer
Lord Jesus, help us to follow your example by being kind to one another. Help us never to feel too highly of ourselves but to realise that as we serve and help each other we are pleasing and serving you. Amen

Song
'When I needed a neighbour, were you there?' (*Junior Praise* 275, *Come and Praise* 65)

Extensions/Curriculum links
- Retell the story in class in another form: as a story board or cartoon.
- Technology: designing a proper suit of new clothes for the Emperor.

46 SIMON SAYS

8-10 mins

Aim
To show that Jesus advice is good advice

Preparation
None.

Age focus
General/Infant

Today we are going to play a game. You know it well. It is called 'Simon Says'. In the game you must only do what Simon says. (*For a larger assembly, ask for a group of volunteers.*)

Simon says stand up.
Sit down.
Simon says raise your arms above your head.
Put them down again.
Simon says put them down again.
Simon says you may sit down.
Simon says - everyone start talking.
Be quiet now everyone!
Simon says stop talking.
(*etc. - then end with*) Now let's see who is left in - put up your hand if you are still in! (*This could catch out the remainder!*)
Simon now says that is the end of the game.

How many of you were caught out? You did what Simon told you to do but also some things he did not tell you to as well. Different people tell you to do different things. Which people do you think you should listen to and obey?

> Your teachers?
> Your parents - of course.
> Your grandparents?
> A policeman - when do you think you should do what a policeman tells you to do?
> If a stranger asks you to go with him, should you obey?
> If someone you don't know asks you to get into a car would you do so?
> If someone asks you to eat a strange sweet, would you do so?

(*Each of these topics could be discussed as appropriate.*)

There is someone we should follow, whose wish we should always try to carry out. Jesus is the best example to follow. His is the best advice of all. In the game we do what Simon says. In life we should do what Jesus says.

Prayer
Lord Jesus, you are the best example anyone can have. Help us to understand what you want us to do. May we learn to do your will.
Amen

Song choices
'He gave me eyes so I could see' (*Junior Praise* 74, *Come and Praise* 18)
'Lord Jesus Christ' (*Junior Praise* 156).

Extensions/Curriculum links
- RE work on stories from the life of Jesus where he asked people to follow him.

47 FOLLOW MY LEADER — 6-8 mins

Aim
To show that Jesus is the best example to follow; (this is best as a class assembly.)

Preparation
None

Age focus
General

Introduction
We are going to start with a short game of 'Follow my leader'.

(Begin by playing 'Follow my leader' with the children in line following you in and out of the tables, round the class-room.)

In that game it was my turn to be the leader. You all had to follow me, going where I went and doing what I did.

As we grow up we have to decide who we would like to follow. It is a good idea to follow the good examples set by older boys and girls or by brothers or sisters. Children also like to follow the example set by their parents, or other grown-ups who care for them.

There is someone else who says 'Follow Me'. That person is Jesus who promises to lead us through our lives. He even said 'I am the way'. Jesus is the best leader to follow.

Reading
Luke Chapter 5 v 27 & 28 (Jesus calls Matthew to follow him.)

Prayer
Lord Jesus, help us as we grow up, to follow you and to do the things you want us to do, for you are the best example of all to follow. You are the best leader. Amen

Song
'I danced in the morning', (*Junior Praise* 91, *Come and Praise* 22)

Extensions/Curriculum links
- RE work on stories from the life of Jesus where he asked people to follow him.

48 TRAFFIC SIGNALS 6-8 mins

Aim
To show that there are times for us to go, times to stop and times for us to be ready.

Age focus
General

Preparation
You need to make some cardboard traffic lights - double thickness so that the lights may be changed by slotting in the appropriate coloured card. This could be done as a class project. The simplest method would be to use circular discs of red, yellow and green paper as visual aids. Alternatively you could make battery powered traffic lights with older children.

Have you been in a car or on a bus recently? Did you look out for the traffic lights? Where they on red? What did the driver have to do? What does the green light tell the driver to do? What about the amber light?

The amber light serves two purposes. When the amber light is on, on its own, the driver knows that the traffic signals will turn to red so he must be ready to stop.

As he is waiting at the lights which are on red, he watches them carefully. When the amber light is lit as well as the red one he can then get ready to go because he knows the lights will soon turn to green.

What would happen if the lights were not working? (*Discuss with the children* - e.g. All the cars might stop, causing long queues to form because the drivers are afraid to go, or the traffic might decide to go in both directions at the same time and so cause a crash.)

Isn't it a good job we have traffic signals?

I've made a set out of cardboard. (*Demonstrate.*) Although we are not driving motor cars in our school and lessons, there are times when we should stop, times for us to go and times for us to be ready.

(*Set the traffic signals to red.*) When do you think we should stop? (*Answer*) When the teacher asks us to listen, we should stop what we are doing, or if we are beginning to have a quarrel with someone in the class - we should stop.

(*Set the traffic signals to green.*) When do you think we should go? (*Answer*) When we are told to get on with our work, or if we see someone who needs help.

(*Set the traffic signals to amber.*) When do you think we should be ready? (*Answer*) Always be ready to listen to instructions, or to lend a helping hand.

Jesus says to his followers, 'Go - go and do to other people what you would like them to do to you.' (*See Luke Chapter 10 v 30 to 37, the Parable of the Good Samaritan.*)

He tells us, also, to be 'ready' - ready to say a kind helpful word to others who may need our help.

He also tells us to 'stop' worrying because he is our friend who is always willing to help us. (*See Matthew Chapter 6 v 34.*)

Prayer
Father God, help us to know when we should go and when we should stop. May we always be ready to help people who are not as fortunate as we are, for in helping others we are serving you. Amen

Song choices
'Two little eyes' (*Junior Praise*: 262)
'He gave me eyes so I could see' (*Junior Praise* 74, *Come and Praise* 18)

Extensions/Curriculum links
- Technology: projects on making signals and alarms.
- RE: Retelling the story of the Good Samaritan in own words.

49 SNAKES AND LADDERS — 6-8 mins — RS21

Aim
To show that life has its ups and downs.

Age focus
General

Preparation
Use Resource Sheet 21 as an OHT to make a snakes and ladders board to be used in front of the whole school; with a small group a real board can be used. You will also need a dice and counters.

Do you know how to play Snakes and Ladders? Good, well let's play a game. (*A small group of children could take turns shaking the dice and moving the counters.*) I will stick the pin in the right square on the board so that you will all be able to see where we are up to. Remember, if we land on a square with the bottom of a ladder in it we then shoot straight to the top. But if we land on a square where there is a snake's head then we are gobbled up by the snake and have to move all the way down to the square where the snake's tail finishes.

(*Play the game for a bit. To keep it short, ensure that the numbers 3, 2, 1 or 4 are shaken.*) That was an exciting game - all about ups and downs. As you get older you will find out that life itself is like a game of snakes and ladders. We all have our ups and downs. One day everything may seem to go well, we feel very happy and it is like going up a ladder in the game. Sometimes, though, we may have an 'off' day - we may get our work wrong. Something may happen to make us feel sad, we may not be feeling very well. We feel on these days that we have slipped all the way down a snake.

Jesus wants us to know that he will be with us during our ups and our downs if we will ask him. He promises his followers, 'I am with you always.' (*See Matthew Chapter 28 v 20.*)

Prayer
Lord Jesus, we ask you to be with us during our good days but also when we are feeling down. Help us to know that we are always in your hands. Amen

Song choices
'One more step along the world I go' (*Junior Praise* 188, *Come and Praise* 47)
'Be bold, be strong for the Lord God is with you' (*Junior Praise* 14)
'The journey of life' (*Come and Praise* 45)

Extensions/Curriculum links:
• Technology: children can design their own boards and game pieces.

50 THE LORD'S PRAYER

6-8 mins

Aim
To explain the meaning of the Lord's Prayer

Preparation
None

Age focus
General

One day the followers of Jesus heard him praying to his Heavenly Father. This is the prayer he said:

> Our Father in heaven,
> May your name be honoured,
> May your kingdom come.
> May your will be done on earth
> as it is in heaven.
> Give us today the food we need.
> Forgive us the wrongs we have done,
> As we forgive the wrongs
> that others have done to us.
> Do not bring us to hard testing,
> but keep us safe from the evil one.
> (Matthew Chapter 6 v 9 to 13.)

You may also know the Lord's prayer in the traditional version.

> Our Father, who art in heaven,
> Hallowed be Thy name.
> Thy kingdom come, Thy will be done
> On earth as it is in heaven.
> Give us this day our daily bread,
> And forgive us our trespasses,
> As we forgive those who trespass against us.
> Lead us not into temptation
> But deliver us from evil.
> For Thine is the kingdom.
> The power and the glory,
> For ever and ever. Amen.

You may find some of this prayer a little difficult to understand so here is a much easier form:

> Dear Father in heaven!
> We love you!
> We want you to be happy.
> Please may we have, each day, the things we need.
> We are sorry that sometimes we make mistakes.
> Help us to love and care for each other
> Because you love each of us.
> Please look after us and keep us safe always.
> Thank you dear God.
> We think you are wonderful! Amen.

Jesus taught his disciples this prayer and wants us to use it too. Jesus tells us that when we say our prayers we should be happy, (*Matthew Chapter 6 v 16*) and we should mean what we say. (*Matthew Chapter 6 v 7*)

As we use this prayer today let us try to mean every word. (*Say the Lord's Prayer together.*)

Hymn choices
'Thank you for every new good morning' (*Junior Praise* 230)
'Thank you Lord for this fine day' (*Junior Praise* 232)
'All things bright and beautiful' (*Junior Praise* 6, *Come and Praise* 3)
A musical setting to the Lord's prayer can be found at No. 51 in Come and Praise.

Extensions/Curriculum links
- Decorated classroom display of different versions of the Lord's Prayer.

51 HOUSES

8-10 mins   **RS22**

Aim
To explain that a church is God's house.

Preparation
You need Resource Sheet 22 as an OHT.

Age focus
General

Throughout the world people live in all sorts of different types of houses. I want to show you some. (*Show OHT.*) Can you tell me who lives in each house?

- **Castle** This is a very strong house, built in the middle ages days. Knights and their servants used to live in houses like these.
- **Palace** These are very elaborate houses fit for kings, queens, princes and princesses to live in. Can anyone tell me the name of the palace where our present Queen Elizabeth lives?
- **Caravan** This might be either a holiday home, or it might be used all the time by someone who travels around to live.
- **Wigwam** What do you call the people who used to live in 'houses' like this? North American Indians. Because these people didn't stay in one place for very long they needed a home made of material so that it could be quickly taken down when they had to move on. Nowadays most North American Indians live in modern houses.
- **Igloo** The Eskimo people used to live in houses like this. Living as they do in a very cold part of the world, in the past they used to make their houses out of blocks of ice without any risk of the sun melting them. These days eskimos live in more modern houses.
- **Churches** Finally let us look at pictures of different churches, (mosques, temples etc.). A church is also called a 'house of God'. What sort of people would you expect to find in a church? Christian people go to church to pray to God, to thank him for his love, to sing his praises and to learn more about God and his Son, Jesus.

Optional conclusion
Jesus was very sad once when he found the people spoiling God's House. They had made it into a sort of market place. He said to them that God wanted his house to be a house of prayer but that the people had made it into a 'den of thieves'. (*See Matthew Chapter 21 v 13.*)

Prayer
Thank you Heavenly Father for the safety and comfort of our homes and for all who love and care for us. Help us to take care of our homes and to respect other people's property. Amen

Song choices
'For the beauty of the earth' (*Junior Praise* 48, *Come and Praise* 11)
'The King of Love my Shepherd is' (*Come and Praise* 54)

Extensions/Curriculum links
- Technology: make model houses for various purposes and climates.
- RE: visit a church or other religious building.

52 WHOSE JOB IS IT?

6-8 mins — **RS23**

Aim
To encourage class responsibility

Age focus
General/Infant

Preparation
You need Resource Sheet 23 as an OHT or copymaster; it will be useful also to have a blank OHT or flipchart sheet for recording suggestions.

Today's story is about four people with silly names: Mr Everybody, Mr Somebody, Mr Anybody and Mr Nobody. Here they are. (*Show pictures.*)

Story
There was an important job to be done and Everybody was sure that Somebody would do it. Anybody could have done it, but Nobody did it. Somebody got angry about that because it was Everyody's job. Everbody thought Anybody could do it. It ended up that Everybody blamed Somebody when Nobody did what Anybody could have done!

Here in our classroom there are jobs which Everybody should do. Can you think what they are? (*List them on an OHT or flipchart.*) e.g.
- Keeping the library corner and shelves tidy
- Keeping the sand-pit tidy.
- Tidying the chairs and tables.
- Closing the door if you are last into the classroom or last to leave it.

In these ways Everybody has a job to do. When everyone does their share of the work, the classroom is kept neat and tidy, we will know that everything is in its right place and Everybody will be happy.

Jesus told his friends that he had a very special job for Everybody to do. It is to spread around the good news of God's love.

Readings
Mark Chapter 16 v 14 & 15 (Jesus' special instruction to his disciples); Matthew Chapter 25 v 34 to 40

Prayer
Help us all, dear Lord, to play our part in keeping our classroom and school tidy. May we never just leave these important jobs to other people. Help us, too, to obey your command to tell others of your love for them, for in so doing we are helping to make the world a better, happier place for Everybody. Amen

Song
'When I needed a neighbour' (*Junior Praise* 275, *Come and Praise* 65)

Extensions/Curriculum links
- Groups of children can retell the story or make up their own story about the characters in an illustrated 'Mr Men' style book, using illustrations from the resource sheet for covers or pictures.

53 TEDDY BEARS

15-20 mins

Aim
To show that Jesus is our friend

Age focus
General/Infant

Preparation
Ask the children who have teddy bears to bring them in to school for a display and/or make a frieze from paper cut-outs of teddy bears. (This could be done beforehand as an art project.) Perhaps bring in a teddy bear of your own! A selection of poems about teddy bears to read out could be useful.

How many of you have a best friend? I'm not going to ask you who your very best friend is because I expect you have lots of friends and it would be difficult to choose just one.

There is a saying that 'a man's best friend is his dog'. Why do you think this is so?
(*Invite answers such as the following:*)
Because a dog is faithful.
A dog always comes when he is called.
A dog does what he is told to do.
My dog always waits patiently when I am away and looks forward to my coming home from school.
My dog loves to play games with me.
My dog never quarrels like my brother or sister!
(*and so on.*)

How many of you have a pet dog? Have you taught it to do any tricks? tell us about them. (*Invite suggestions.*)

Many of you have brought in a teddy bear to show us and I'm sure you look upon your teddy as a very special friend. (*Invite some children to show their teddy bears*.)
Why do you like it?
Who gave it to you?
Where do you keep it?
Have you given your teddy bear a special name?
Optional) This is my very own teddy bear which I have had since I was … years old. (T*ell the children something about your bear.*)

Most children like to have a teddy bear which they treasure and keep for many years until they themselves are grown up and have children of their own.

Teddy bears are kept usually in a bedroom because they are looked upon as a friend who will keep their owner safe when they are asleep.

Here is a very old rhyme which children used to say as they skipped:
   Teddy bear, teddy bear turn around,
   Teddy bear, teddy bear touch the ground,
   Teddy bear, teddy bear go up stairs,
   Teddy bear, teddy bear say your prayers,
   Teddy bear, teddy bear turn off the light,
   Teddy bear, teddy bear say good-night.
(*Here other poems about teddy bears can be read out.*)

We have been thinking today about our best friends. Your best friend may well be a member of your class. It could be that you look upon your pet dog as a very good friend. Teddy bears give so much love and friendship that to some people they are almost real.

There is someone who will give us all the love, friendship and safety we need. I'm talking now about Jesus who has promised to be our Friend and who wants us to be his friends. (*See John 15v 14 and 15.*)

Prayer
Lord Jesus, we thank you that you have promised to be a friend to each one of us. We

ask you to take care of us, to keep us safe and help us to be your friends too. Amen

Song choices
'Jesus is a friend of mine' (*Junior Praise* 136)
'Jesus' love is very wonderful' (*Junior Praise* 139)
'Jesus Christ is here' (*Come and Praise* 26)

Extension/Curriculum links
- English: making up teddy bear poems or poems about pet dogs.
- Art: project on bears.

54 LISTEN!

6-8 mins

Aim
To explain how we can 'listen' to Jesus

Age focus
General/Infant

Preparation
Collect the following objects beforehand: a bell, a jug of water and a cup, musical box, a mouth organ or other small wind instrument, a piece of paper.

Today we are going to play a game. In a moment I will ask you all to close your eyes. While your eyes are closed I will make some noises. When I ask you to open your eyes again I hope you will be able to tell me what sounds you heard. Now close your eyes.

Listen now to these sounds, but don't say anything yet.
1. Small bell ringing.
2. Hands clapping.
3. Water being poured into a jug.
4. Musical box.
5. Mouth organ.
6. Paper rustling.

Now open your eyes and tell me what you heard.

Isn't it strange that no one said they heard me speaking! (*Or* I'm glad you also said you heard me speaking).

Now we will play the game again but this time I will not be making any sounds myself. See if you can hear any noises. Close your eyes.

(Hopefully the children will hear a range of sounds such as a clock ticking, the wind outside, leaves rustling on the trees, a dog barking, a chair squeaking, a motor car passing etc.)

Open your eyes again. You had to listen very hard then! What did you hear?

Sometimes we have to train our ears to hear, for example, when you are being told something very important at school or when your parents are telling you something. When Jesus was teaching one day, he said to the people, 'listen! If you have ears then you should use them!' (*Mark Chapter 4 v 9.*)

We, too, should listen to what Jesus has to say to us for as we read the Bible or listen to the stories of Jesus he is actually speaking to us through his word.

Prayer
We thank you, Heavenly Father, for giving us eyes to see and ears to hear. We think today of people who are not as fortunate as we are, who cannot see or cannot hear. Help them, O God, to overcome their difficulties so that they will be able to live happy, useful lives. For our part, Lord, help us to use our eyes to read your word and as we do so, help us to realise that you are speaking to us. In this way help us to hear what you have to say to us. Amen

Song choices
'Two little eyes to look to God, two little ears to hear his word' (*Junior Praise* 262)
'He gave me eyes so I could see' (*Junior Praise* 74, *Come and Praise* 18)
'A still small voice' (*Come and Praise* 96)

Extensions/Curriculum links
- Science work on sounds and the senses.
- 'Hearing' poems in which every verse starts 'I can hear…'

55 THANK YOU

6-8 mins

Aim
To encourage courtesy and gratitude

Age focus
General

Preparation
You need a 'Thank You' card.

One day Jesus was going into a village when he was met by ten men who all had a terrible skin disease. They asked Jesus to have pity on them. Jesus was very sorry for them and decided to help. He said that they should first go and show themselves to the priest, but on the way there something wonderful happened. They were all made well again. Jesus had healed them. One of the ten, when he discovered he had been healed went back to find Jesus and said, 'Thank You!' Sadly the other nine did not bother. (*Luke Chapter 17 v 11-19.*)

Do you always remember to say thank you? Let us make a list of the times when we should say thank you.
- Thank you to the person who gives you your breakfast.
- Thank you to the one who brings you to school.
- Thank you to the driver as you get off the school bus.
- Thank you to the 'lollipop lady' for seeing you safely across the road.
- Thank you to your friend for letting you use his/her pencil.
- Thank you to the dinner lady for serving your lunch.
- Thank you to parents for buying you sweets.
- Thank you to parents for taking you on holiday.
    etc.

Sometimes it is a good idea to send a thank you card like this one if someone has been especially kind, say, in inviting you to a party.

We should also remember, like the man in the story, to say thank you to Jesus for his love and care.

Prayer
Lord Jesus, we want to say thank you for all your kindness and love. Thank you for this new day, thank you for all our friends, thank you for our homes and those who care for us, thank you for the lessons we learn and the games we play. Help us always to be grateful and to show this by saying 'Thank You!' Amen

Song choices
'Thank you Lord for this fine day' (*Junior Praise* 232, *Come and Praise* 32)
'Thank you for every new good morning' (*Junior Praise* 230)
'Heavenly Father may Thy blessing' (*Come and Praise* 62)

Extensions/Curriculum links
- Design and display Thank You cards for Jesus.

56 BULLIES

6-8 mins

Aim
To encourage respect for others

Age focus
General/Junior

Preparation
None

Introduction
No one likes being bullied. It is very sad when someone, usually quite big, takes an unfair advantage of someone smaller. Of course you know very well that we do not allow bullying in our school.

Today's story is about a bully and what happened to him.

The story of David and Goliath
David was the youngest son of his father Jesse. All his brothers had gone to fight for their country but David had to remain at home looking after the sheep because he was too young to join the army. The Israelites were being attacked by their enemies the Philistines. One day, one of the Philistines named Goliath started taunting the Israelites. He was a giant of a man, nearly three metres tall, (nine feet). He wore bronze armour and carried a huge bronze shield and a very heavy spear. Goliath started calling the Israelites names and challenged them to fight him but the Israelites were terrified and no-one dared to take up the challenge. The taunts went on for forty days.

It so happened that young David came to the battle front with food for his brothers. When he heard of the challenge he said to the Israelite King, Saul, 'Your majesty, let no-one be afraid, I will go and fight him! The Lord saved me from lions and bears when I was looking after my father's sheep, he will also save me from this Philistine.'

Although King Saul was very reluctant to let a young lad fight against this giant of a man, he eventually agreed. 'All right,' said Saul, 'and the Lord be with you.'

The Philistine started walking towards David, with his shield bearer walking in front of him. He kept coming closer. When he got a good look at David and saw that he had no armour, no sword, no spear or shield and that he was just a young boy, he swaggered and said, 'Do you think I am a dog? Come on then, I will give your body to the birds and animals to eat.'

To this David replied, 'You come to me with sword, spear and javelin but I come in the name of the Lord.'

With that, David stooped down and chose five smooth pebbles from the brook. He put one of the small stones into his home-made sling and sent the stone flying towards Goliath. It struck the Philistine on the forehead. The giant fell, face down to the ground. When the Philistines saw that their hero was dead they all fled for their lives.

As for David, he eventually became King of the Israelite people after King Saul.

One lesson we can learn from this story is that Goliath was a bully who in the end got what he deserved. Bullies usually pick on people much smaller than themselves because they are not brave enough to challenge someone their own size. We should also remember, like David, that we can always ask the Lord to help us with our problems.

Prayer
Help us, Lord, to be always loving and kind towards other people. Help us, also, to

remember that unkind words only bring unhappiness to everyone. Amen

Song choices
'Only a boy called David' (*Junior Praise* 90)
'Be bold, be strong for the Lord God is with you' (*Junior Praise* 14)
'When a knight won his spurs' (*Come and Praise* 50)

Extensions/Curriculum links
- Retell the story as a class play.
- Make scale models/wall displays of David and Goliath.

57 GREEN CROSS CODE — 8-10 mins

Aim
To show that we are all greatly valued by God

Age focus
General

Preparation
Make a large green cross. Have a blank OHT or flipchart sheet for recording the code.

Introduction
Do you know what this means? (*Show Green Cross*). It is the symbol of the Green Cross Code. How many of you know the Green Cross Code? (*Discuss*.)

Let's write up the code. (*With the help of the children, write up the Green Cross Code*.)
1 First find a safe place to cross. then stop.
2 Stand on the pavement near the kerb.
3 Look all around for traffic and listen.
4 If traffic is coming, let it pass. Look all around again.
5 When there is no traffic near, walk straight across the road.
6 Keep looking and listening for traffic while you cross.

When it is 'home time' at the end of the school day, you all know what arrangements have been made for you to get home. It is very important that you remember what you have been told to do and not go wandering off on your own.

Susan did a silly thing one day. Her mother had said she would be there to meet her outside the school gate but for some reason she had not turned up.

'Well,' thought Susan, 'I know the way home, I'm sure I can manage,' so she set off on her own. After a while she had to cross a busy main road but Susan wasn't worried, she knew the kerb drill, she had learned the Green Cross Code: 'At the kerb, stop! Look right, look left, look right again and if there is nothing coming walk straight across the road. Keep looking and listening as you walk across the road.'

Susan stopped at the kerb and waited for a break in the traffic. Then she heard a voice which said: 'The little girl in the blue anorak can cross the road safely now'. Having heard the voice, she checked again that the road was clear and crossed over. No sooner had she reached the other side than she came face to face with her mother.

'I'm sorry I was a little late, Susan, but you should have waited for me at school, you know it is very dangerous crossing the main road.'

'It was quite safe,' said Susan, 'because God told me I could cross.'

Her mum was very puzzled by this but listened while Susan told her how the mystery voice had said the little girl in the blue anorak could cross the road safely now. 'It must have been God!' said Susan. Just then, Susan's mother noticed, parked in a side road, a police car with a loud speaker. It must have been the policeman who spoke to Susan.

God doesn't usually speak to people like that, does he! Anyway, if it had been God he wouldn't have said, 'The little girl in the blue anorak...', he would have called her name - Susan.

God does know each of us by name and loves us and cares for us and, yes, he may well speak to us but does so through his word, the Bible, or through our consciences - the quiet little voice inside us which tells us whether we are doing the right thing or not.

Prayer
We want to thank you again, Heavenly Father, for your love and for taking care of us. Thank you that you know all our names, that we are, each one, valuable to you. Help us to do the things you want us to do and so make the world a happier place. Amen

Song choices
'Father lead me day by day' (*Junior Praise* 43)
'One more step along the world I go (*Junior Praise* 188, *Come and Praise* 47)

Extensions/Curriculum links
- Ensure that every child in the school knows the Green Cross Code. Create classroom displays and practice drills if need be.

58 FAST AND SLOW

6-8 mins

Aim
To encourage the children to take care with their work

Preparation
None

Age focus
General

Do any of you keep a pet tortoise? How does it walk? Does it walk fast or slowly? Which do you think could run fastest - a tortoise or a hare?

Here is a very old story by a man called Aesop who lived in Egypt even before the time of Jesus. This story is called 'The Hare and the Tortoise'.

'A hare was always making fun of a tortoise because it could only walk very slowly. 'Hurry up, slowcoach,' the hare would shout.

One day the tortoise decided that he would teach the hare a lesson, so he challenged him to a race.

The hare fell about laughing. 'A race with you,' he jeered, 'I would finish before you had even crossed the starting line!'

'We'll see,' said the tortoise, and so the race began. The hare quickly sprang into the lead and disappeared down the path. Meanwhile the tortoise just went along at his steady pace.

Before long the hare decided to stop and have a rest because he was so far in front. 'It will take the tortoise hours to catch up with me,' he said. With that, the hare fell asleep, intending just to have a quick nap. The tortoise kept plodding steadily on. When the hare awoke with a start it was to see the tortoise crossing the finishing line ahead of him.

Aesop said that the moral of his story is: 'Slow and steady wins the race'.

In our school work we often find that people who rush their work manage to get it all wrong, whilst those who quietly and steadily get carefully on with it finish up by doing very good work. So you see, Aesop had a message for us to think about.

Jesus, also, taught his disciples that when they start doing a job they should keep steadily on with it.

For older pupils
Compare Luke Chapter 9 v 62, 'He who puts his hand to the plough and turns back is not fit for the Kingdom of God', with Hebrews Chapter 12 v 1 & 2, 'Run with patience...looking to Jesus.'

Prayer
Help us, Lord, to do our best with our work, to be patient and careful and help us to remember that nothing but the very best will do for you! Amen

Song choices
'Father I place into your hands' (*Junior Praise* 42)
'The journey of life' (*Come and Praise* 45)

Extensions/Curriculum links
- English: explore Aesop's fables further with the children.
- Younger children could present the story as a wall display, perhaps creating simple maps of the course for infant geography skills.

59 THE LION'S THORN

6-8 mins

Aim
To show that good deeds are often rewarded.

Preparation
None

Age focus
General

Here is a story which was first told many years ago, even before the time of Jesus. It is about Androcles and the Lion.

There was once a slave named Androcles whose master ill-treated him so much that Androcles could not stand it any longer and decided to run away into the forest. Before long he came across a roaring lion which at first terrified him. Then he saw that the lion was, in fact, crying from pain.

As Androcles went up to the lion it put out its paw and Androcles saw a large thorn in one of the lion's toes. Bravely he pulled it out. The lion was so grateful that it licked Androcles' hand and led him to a cave in the forest. Here they lived together for some time, but one day as Androcles and the lion were hunting together they were both captured, taken to the city and put into a circus. In order to entertain the Emperor they first starved the lion for a few days, making him very hungry.

Then they made Androcles go into the circus ring with the fierce lion. With a terrible roar the lion bounded towards the man but when it saw his friend Androcles, it stopped, rolled over and licked Androcles' hand.

The Emperor was so impressed with this unusual sight that he sent for Androcles who told the emperor the whole story. The Emperor set Androcles free and also arranged for the lion to be taken back to the forest.

Aesop, who first told this story, said that it teaches us that a good deed never goes unrewarded.

If we are kind, helpful and respectful to other people it is very likely that they, too, will treat us well. Jesus said, 'Do to others as you would have them do to you.' (*See Matthew Chapter 7 v 12.*)

Prayer
Help us always to be kind helpful and friendly to other people, dear God, because you yourself are a loving Father and we want everyone to know about your love. Amen

Song choices
'He gave me eyes so I could see' (*Junior Praise* 74)
'Make me a channel of your peace' (*Junior Praise* 161, *Come and Praise* 161)

Extensions/Curriculum links
- English: explore Aesop's fables with the children further.

60 LION AND MOUSE

6-8 mins

Aim
To show that kindness is often rewarded.

Preparation
None

Age focus
General

Here is another story first told by Aesop. It is about a lion and a mouse.

One day a lion lay asleep when a tiny mouse scampered across his nose. This woke the lion and made him very angry. He quickly trapped the little mouse under his great paw and was about to kill him, when he heard the mouse squeak, 'Please forgive me your majesty. Don't kill me. If you let me live I promise that one day I will do you a good turn to pay back your kindness.'

The great lion was amused that the tiny mouse should think that he could possibly help in any way so he decided to let his prisoner go.

A few days later, the lion was prowling in the forest when he got caught in a net which hunters had set to trap him. Though he struggled and struggled, the mighty lion could not get free, so he began to roar as loudly as he could. The little mouse heard him, recognised his voice and came scurrying to help.

'Good day, your majesty,' the mouse said. 'This is my chance to repay your kindness to me.'

The mouse then began to gnaw at the ropes with his tiny, sharp teeth until before long a large hole was made through which the lion was able to escape.

Aesop said the story shows that no kind act, however small, is ever wasted. We usually find that when we are kind to someone, they will look for an opportunity to be kind to us. Jesus said that we should even be kind to our enemies and that we should pray for them. (*See Matthew Chapter 5 v 44.*)

Prayer
O God, may we never repay a bad turn with a bad turn. Help us to be kind and thoughtful in our dealings with everyone, for in this way we will be helping to make the world the sort of place you want it to be. Amen

Song choices
'When I needed a neighbour, were you there' (*Junior Praise* 275, *Come and Praise* 65)
'I will make you fishers of men' (*Junior Praise* 123)

Extensions/Curriculum links
- Technology: design a trap to catch a particular kind of animal without harming it.

61 THE CROOKED MAN 6-8 mins RS24

Aim
To show that there is a lot of good in the world.

Preparation
None but you may like to use Resource Sheet 24 as an OHT.

Age focus
General

Do you know this poem? (*Show poem and picture as an OHT if you like.*)
> There was a crooked man
> Who walked a crooked mile,
> He found a crooked sixpence
> Against a crooked stile.
> He bought a crooked cat,
> Which caught a crooked mouse
> And they all lived together
> In a little crooked house.

In that well-known poem everything is crooked - the man (*like this picture*), the sixpence, the stile, the cat, the mouse, the house, even the mile they walked was crooked.

Some people say that the world is a crooked place. When people tell lies and do cruel things then they are being crooked. But there is so much that is good, so many kind people and the world itself is very beautiful. We must all do what we can to prevent it becoming crooked. By the sort of lives we live, we can help make it a better place. Through the words we speak, we can help others to realise that God loves us all. Let us always look for the good in people and in the world.

Prayer
We thank you, Heavenly Father, for making the world such a wonderful place. May we never do anything to spoil its beauty. May there be nothing crooked in our lives. Help us always to be loving and kind. Amen

Song choices
'For the beauty of the earth' (*Junior Praise* 48, *Come and Praise* 11)
'All things bright and beautiful' (*Junior Praise* 6, *Come and Praise* 3)
'Who put the colours in the rainbow' (*Junior Praise* 288, *Come and Praise* 12)
'God who made the earth' (*Junior Praise* 63, *Come and Praise* 10)
'Stand up, clap hands, shout thank you Lord' (*Junior Praise* 225)

Extensions/Curriculum links
- English: inventing 'crooked' poems modelled on this one e.g. 'There was a crooked - , who…
- Art: illustrating the whole poem for a wall picture.

62 I SPY

8-10 mins

Aim
To help other people to form good impressions.

Age focus
General

Preparation
You need to arrange a display of *I Spy* books (published by Michelin Tyres PLC, Davy House, Lyon Road, Harrow, Middlesex HA1 2DQ)

Probably one of the first games you ever played was called I Spy. Let's try it now. (*Play I Spy for a few minutes*.)

I Spy will always be a popular game. Now I'd like to show you some books. they are very useful for taking on holiday or with you when you go on a journey. They are called *I Spy* books. They tell you what sorts of things to look out for as you go along. (*Show the children examples of I Spy books*.)

When we travel about, if we are observant, we will spy or spot lots of interesting things. But have you ever thought that other people spy or spot us too?

When they spy or spot us they may be able to tell which school we belong to. How to you think they could do that? (*Ask for suggestions* e.g. They may see us coming out of school. They may see our school uniform. They may spot our school badge. etc.)

I hope they will also spy that we are well-behaved, kind to others, friendly, helpful and well-mannered. In these ways others should spy that we belong to this school.

Jesus teaches us that we should try to live in such a way that people will see (spy) the good things we do. (*See Matthew 5 v 16*: 'Let your light so shine before others that they may see your good deeds and give glory to God.')

Prayer
Dear God, help us day by day to be loving, kind and helpful so that when others see us they will know that we are trying to live the way Jesus taught us. Amen

Song choices
'Father, lead me day by day' (*Junior Praise* 43)
'When I needed a neighbour were you there?' (*Junior Praise* 275, *Come and Praise* 65)

Extensions/Curriculum links
• RE: Stories in the New Testament where people spotted Jesus. What was he doing at the time? (*Matthew 2 v 11, Matthew 9 v 2, Matthew 12 v 1, Matthew 14 v 13 and 14, Matthew 14 v 26, Mark 11 v 8, Luke 10 v 25, Luke 19 v 5, Luke 22 v 61*)

63 FIVE POUND NOTE

6-8 mins

Theme
To help other people to form good impressions.

Age focus
General

Preparation
You need a five pound note.

I'm sure you will recognise this. (*Show the note.*) It is a five pound note. What is the best way of getting money? (*Discuss.*)
(*Answer*) By working hard for it!

Why do we need money? (*Again discuss.*)
(*Answer*) So that we can buy things from the shops.

This is only a piece of paper. How do I know it is worth five pound? (*Discuss.*)

It is because of what is printed on it. The person in charge of the Bank of England has printed a promise on this piece of paper. It says:

'I promise to pay the bearer, on demand, the sum of five pounds.' It is my five pound note - I am the bearer, and because he has made me a promise, I can take it into a shop and exchange it for food, clothes or anything else to the value of five pounds. I'm glad he keeps his promise.

How many of you have recently made a promise? What did you promise? What sort of things could you promise to do? Here are some suggestions:
  Promise to keep your bedrooms tidy!
  Promise to help to dry the dishes.
  Promise to help with the gardening.
  Promise to be kind to your younger brother or sister.
  Promise me that you will listen carefully to what I tell you.

We are all good at making promises. What is it that is much more difficult? Answer: Keeping them.

God has made us some wonderful promises and he always keeps them. He promises that if we say we are sorry when we do wrong, he will forgive us. (*See 1 John Chapter 1 v 9.*) Jesus promises that he will never leave us. (*See Matthew Chapter 28 v 20.*)

Prayer
Dear Heavenly Father we are sorry that sometimes we do things which we ought not to do and we say things which upset other people. Thank you for your promise to forgive. Thank you Lord Jesus for promising to be with us always. Help us to keep the promises we make to other people. Amen

Song choices
'Father lead me day by day' (*Junior Praise* 43)
'When the road is deep and rough' (*Junior Praise* 279)
'He who would valiant be' (*Come and Praise* 44)

Extensions/Curriculum links
- History: find out about the history of money and banks.

64 BADGES

8-12 mins

Aim
To encourage children to feel they belong

Age focus
General/Junior

Preparation
You need to create a display of badges, using badges brought in by the children. Ensure that many of them relate to clubs and organisations.

First of all, thank you to all the children who have brought in badges for us to see. I'm going to ask them in turn to say what their badge is and how they came to get it. e.g.
- Brownies
- Cub Scouts
- Porpoise Club
- National Trust
- Y.O.C. (Young Ornithologists Club)
- World Wildlife Fund
- St. John's Ambulance
- Scripture Union
- Also military badges or football club badges.

Most badges show that the wearer belongs to that particular club. It is good to belong to a club, to feel that you have lots of friends who have something in common with you.

I hope you are all pleased to wear the school badge and that all the members of our school are your friends. It is good to belong to (*Name of your school*) school.

People we meet are able to see that we belong to this school by the badge we wear.
They should also be able to see that we are followers of the Lord Jesus even though we don't wear a badge.

They should be able to tell because we are loving, kind and helpful. Jesus said, 'Others will be able to see that you are my friends when you have love for one another.' (*See John Chapter 13 v 35.*)

Prayer
We thank you, Lord, for the school we belong to and the many friends we have here. Help us to be loving and kind to one another, for in this way we are doing your will. Amen

Song choices
'He's got the whole world in his hands' (*Junior Praise* 78, *Come and Praise* 19)
'Jesus love is very wonderful' (*Junior Praise* 139)

Extensions/Curriculum links
- Design a new badge for the school.

65 HOBBIES

8-15 mins

Aim
To encourage reliability and persistence

Age focus
General/Junior

Preparation
Ask children in the class to bring in items that relate to particular hobbies. You can either create a hobbies display or children can bring along items to talk about during the assembly.

Who knows what a hobby is? Who has a hobby? (*Discuss.*)

A hobby is a favourite pastime - something you enjoy doing in your spare time. You will see from our exhibition that many members of our class (school) have interesting hobbies. I'm going to ask some of you to tell us about your particular hobby.

How long have you been interested in it? Why do you like it? (*Ask the children to talk about the hobby.*)

Hobbies could include the following:
  Stamp collecting
  Model making
  Baking/cooking
  Sewing
  Knitting
  Coin collecting
  Reading
  Video/computer games
  War games
  Swimming
  Cycling   etc.

It is a very good idea to have a hobby in which you can really get involved. Many young people continue with their hobby even after they have grown up. Sadly, however, many people give up or keep changing their interests. They start collecting stamps then change to collecting something different. Then they begin to make a model but never finish it. We get more pleasure out of our hobbies the more time and effort we put in to them. So don't give up.

Following Jesus should be more than a hobby which we eventually give up. Jesus wants, as his followers, those who are going to be reliable - people who stick at it.   (*See Luke Chapter 9 v 62.*)

Prayer
Thank you Lord for our hobbies and for the pleasure they give to us. Help us to understand that the more effort we put in the more satisfying our hobby will be. Even though we may get tired of our hobbies, may we never get tired of following you. Amen

Song choices
'I want to walk with Jesus Christ' (*Junior Praise* 124)
'Lord of the dance' (*Junior Praise* 91, *Come and Praise* 22)

Extensions/Curriculum links
• Classroom display with factual writing about hobbies.

66 KING MIDAS

6-8 mins — **RS25**

Aim
Don't be greedy.

Age focus
General

Preparation
None is required, but this story can be effectively dramatised by getting your class to prepare in advance items of artificial fruit sprayed with gold paint, or diagrams of fruit painted gold. You can use Resource Sheet 25a and b as templates for this activity.

This story is about an ancient king named Midas. King Midas was very wealthy but also very greedy. He wasn't satisfied with all the treasure he possessed but wanted more and more.

One day, a prisoner named Silenus was brought to King Midas. Silenus entertained the king for five whole days at the end of which the king was so pleased that he set the prisoner free. Silenus was very grateful and, in return, he said he would arrange for King Midas to have anything he wanted. The king, being very greedy, asked that anything he touched would be turned to gold. 'Your wish is granted,' said Silenus.

King Midas was absolutely delighted - he touched his chair and immediately it turned to gold. He touched a table and other items of furniture and they turned to gold. The stones he touched turned to gold, even the carpets and the flowers. 'How happy I am, I shall be the richest person in the whole world. I can have anything I want,' said King Midas.

But then he felt hungry! He picked up an apple - like this one (*show gold fruit*) - and it turned to gold. He picked up a pear. It, too, turned to gold. His glass of wine turned to solid gold. Midas now begged to be released from his wish because he was afraid he would die of hunger and thirst.

One of his advisers then told him of a certain river. 'If you go there and wash yourself in the river you will be cured,' he said. Midas obeyed and was immediately rid of the golden touch, but to this day the sands of that river are a bright golden colour!

This story teaches us to be satisfied with what we have and not to be greedy. There are more important things than gold and wealth. What good is it if we have all the wealth in the world but don't have good health and good friends?

God's holy book, the Bible, tells us that there are far more important things to have than gold:
    To be wise is better than having gold.
    To do God's will is better than having gold.
    Believing in God is better than having gold.
(*See Proverbs Chapter 16 v 16; Psalm Chapter 19 v 10; 1 Peter Chapter 1 v 7.*)

Prayer
Teach us, Lord, not to be greedy but give us a desire to help those who are not as fortunate as we are, for you have taught us that when we are helping others we are pleasing you. Amen

Song choices
'The wise may bring their learning' (*Junior Praise* 253, *Come and Praise* 64)
'He gave me eyes so I could see' (*Junior Praise* 74, *Come and Praise* 18)

Extensions/Curriculum links
- Children can make displays of gold objects and include written accounts of the story in the display. Golden fruit can be made using the resource sheets.

67 CLOCKS

6-8 mins   **RS26**

Aim
To show that we must be reliable

Age focus
General

Preparation
Collect several different clocks or use Resource Sheet 26 as an OHT.

How do you know when it is time to get up in a morning?

How do you know when it is time to go to school?
   How do you know when it is playtime?
   How do you know when it is lunch time?
   How do you know when it is home time?
   How do you know when it is time to switch the television on for your favourite programme?

The answer to all these questions is that the clock tells us the time. Isn't it a good job we can rely on clocks!

There are lots of different kinds of clocks. Here are a few for you to see. (*Show clocks or use the OHT.*) Can you think of any other sorts?
(*Ask children to name some clocks e.g.*)
   School clock
   Town Hall clock
   Big Ben
   Wall clocks
   Grandfather clocks
   Grand daughter clocks
   Alarm clocks
   Travel clocks
   Wrist watches
   Pocket watches
   Chiming clocks

We rely on clocks and watches to tell us the right time. But what would it be like if the clock told us the wrong time, if it was too fast, too slow or stopped altogether?

(*Answers along the lines of the following*)
   We may be late for school.
   We could miss the bus.
   We could miss our favourite TV programme etc.

The most important thing about a clock is that it is reliable, that it always tells us exactly the right time because so many people depend on them. In this way we must try to be like clocks. We must do our very best to be reliable so that others can depend on us.

Prayer
Help us to be reliable in all we do, Lord, because so many people depend on us. Help us never to let others down. We thank you Lord that we can always rely on you. Amen

Song choices
'He's got the whole world in his hand' (*Junior Praise* 78, *Come and Praise* 19)
'Jesus' love is very wonderful' (*Junior Praise* 139)

Extensions/Curriculum links
• A class display of different clocks with time telling activities e.g. 'Can you tell what the time is in these different parts of the world'?

68 RED RIDING HOOD — 6-8 mins

Aim
To show that we shouldn't just pretend to be good

Preparation
None

Age focus
General/Infant

Today I want you to listen again to a very well-known children's story - the story of Little Red Riding Hood.

One day little Red Riding Hood was asked by her mother to take a basket of cakes to her granny who lived in a cottage in the woods. 'Be careful to look out for dangerous wolves!' were her mother's last words as little Red Riding Hood set out. When she arrived at the cottage she went straight in to see her granny but today her granny looked rather strange.

'Granny, what big eyes you've got,' said Red Riding Hood.
(*Children may be encouraged to join in the reply.*)
'All the better to see you with!' came the reply.
'But Granny, what big ears you've got,' said the little girl.
'All the better to hear you with,' came the reply.

Then Red Riding Hood noticed her granny's teeth. 'And what big teeth you've got.'
This time the reply came, 'All the better to eat you with!'

The wolf, who had disguised himself in Granny's clothing, having locked Granny in the cupboard, then sprang out of the bed towards Red Riding Hood, who ran, terrified, out of the cottage.

As luck would have it, Red Riding Hood's father, who was a wood-cutter, happened to be passing just then. He rescued Red Riding Hood and Granny 'and they all lived happily ever after'.

In that story the wolf had pretended to be something he really was not. He had pretended to be Red Riding Hood's granny.

Do you ever pretend to be what you really are not?
Do you ever just pretend to be good?
Do you ever pretend you care about other people?
Do you ever pretend you are working hard?
Do you ever pretend you are tidying your bedroom?

It isn't very nice to pretend. It is much better to be genuine - to really care, to try hard to be good, kind and helpful.

Prayer
Lord, you have told us that we should really love each other and not just pretend. Sometimes we do things we know we should not do but we know that you really do love us and that you are always ready to forgive.
Amen

Song choices
'Jesus' love is very wonderful' (*Junior Praise* 139)
'Stand up, clap hands, shout thank you Lord' (*Junior Praise* 225)
'Jesus, good above all other' (*Come and Praise* 23)

Extensions/Curriculum links
• Children can retell the story in a different way: e.g. from the wolf's point of view, from the granny's point of view or as a cartoon.

69 THE RAINBOW

6-8 mins

Aim
To show that we can always rely on God

Age focus
General

Preparation
None, but the assembly can be enlivened by getting children to paint a rainbow or choose seven children to each present a different colour. You might also consider playing a recording of 'Captain Noah and his floating zoo'.

Sometimes when the sun shines brightly during a rain storm, the sun's rays make the tiny droplets of rain shine brilliantly. They form a beautifully coloured arch across the sky. Do you know what this is called? Have you ever seen a rainbow?

A rainbow is said to contain every possible colour, the main ones being: red, orange, yellow, green, blue indigo, violet. On display, today, you have all the colours of the rainbow. (*Show the rainbow display or get the children to display the separate colours.*)

There is a lovely story in the Bible of why the rainbow was first made. It had been raining for forty days and forty nights but at last the rain had stopped. There was so much water that the world was flooded but Noah, his family and the animals were safe inside the ark which God had told Noah to build. Gradually the floods disappeared and Noah was able to step out again on to dry land.

God then promised Noah that he would never again allow the earth to be completely covered by flood waters. 'And as a sign that I will keep my promise I will set my rainbow over the earth.' This wonderful promise we can read in the book of Genesis (Chapter 9 v 8 to 13).

(*Optional*) Let us now listen to this story put to music. (*Play recording of 'Oh! what a wonderful scene', from 'Captain Noah and his floating zoo'.*)

Prayer
Thank you, God, for making such a beautiful world, for painting the world of nature in so many wonderful colours. We thank you, too, that you set your rainbow in the sky to remind us of your faithfulness and your promise to look after us and to protect the earth. May we never do anything to spoil your handiwork but may we do what we can to preserve the countryside. Amen

Song choices
'Colours of day' (*Junior Praise* 28, *Come and Praise* 55)
'Mr Noah built an ark' (*Junior Praise* 167)

Extensions/Curriculum links
- Artwork: Creating rainbows.

70 KEYS
6-8 mins — **RS27**

Aim
To show that hard work is the key to success

Age focus
General

Preparation
Assemble an assortment of keys for display or use Resource Sheet 27 as an OHT

(*Show selection of keys or the OHT*) You may wonder why I'm showing you these keys. As you can see they come in all shapes and sizes.

What is a key used for? Can you suggest some things which need keys? (*Compile a list such as the following. Suggestions could be written on the OHT.*) e.g.
- Padlock; Door lock; Cupboards; Desks; Suitcases; Briefcases; Car doors; Car boots; Dungeons; Safes

Often we use keys to lock things away safely. You may have something valuable in a safe or strong box but if you don't have the key you will not be able to get it out. You won't be able to enjoy the contents of the safe.

Now let me tell you about a different kind of key. I'm sure you all want to do well at school, you want to be successful. There is an imaginary key which opens the 'door' to success. That key is *hard work*. Use this key and I am sure that you will enjoy your lessons even more. Always try to do your best - it is the surest way to succeed.

For older children
There is another type of imaginary key which opens for us the way to God's Heavenly Kingdom. The key for this is *trust*, trust in God.

Reading
Proverbs 3 v 5 and 6

Prayer
Lord God, help us always to remember that the key to success is hard work. help us day by day to put our trust in you so that our work will not be just for our own good but also that it will be pleasing to you. Amen

Song choices
'In our work and in our play' (*Junior Praise* 108)
'Two little eyes to look to God' (*Junior Praise* 262)
'Jesus good above all other' (*Come and Praise* 23)

Extensions/Curriculum links
- D and T: design a security system for a safe.
- English: creative writing using keys as a starter e.g. keys to the magic door.

PRAYERS

Prayers for the end of the day

1 At the close of another day, O God, we come to you to thank you for all we have been able to do. We thank you for your presence during the day which is now past, for your help, guidance and strength. Grant us, Lord, a restful night so that when we awake in the morning we shall be refreshed and renewed for the tasks which lie ahead of us.

2 Lord keep us safe this night, secure from all our fears, may angels guard us while we sleep 'til morning light appears.

3 O Jesus keep us in Thy sight; And guard us through the coming night.

4 Grant us your peace upon our homeward way,
With you began, with you we end our day.

5 Ere I sleep, for every favour
This day showed, by my God,
I will praise my Saviour.

6 Glory to Thee, my God, this night,
For all the blessings of the light,
Keep me, O keep me, King of Kings,
Beneath Thine own almighty wings.

Graces at meal times

1 For food and all your gifts of love,
We give you thanks and praise.
Help us, O Father, in our work,
And bless us all our days.

2 For what we are about to receive may the Lord make us truly thankful.

3 For food and for friendship, we thank you Heavenly Father.

4 Be present at our table Lord
Be hear and everywhere adored.
These children bless and grant that we
May dwell in paradise with Thee.

5 All good gifts around us
Are sent from Heaven above.
Then thank the Lord, O thank the Lord,
For all his love.

6 Thank you for the world so sweet.
Thank you for the food we eat.
Thank you for the birds that sing.
Thank you God for everything.

Benedictions

1 The grace of the Lord Jesus Christ, the love of God and the fellowship of the Holy Spirit be with us all, now and for evermore. Amen

2 The peace of God which passes all our understanding, keep our hearts and minds, through Jesus Christ our Lord. Amen

3 May the peace of God the Father, God the Son and God the Holy Spirit, be with us all, this day and always. Amen

4 May God the Father bless us and all people everywhere and fill our hearts with his peace and goodwill. Amen

5 May the Lord grant us his blessing and fill our hearts with the spirit of truth and peace now and always. Amen

Resource Sheets

85 Resource Sheet 1: The Leopard Learning Assembly Book

Oak

Sycamore

Chestnut

Fir

Apple

Poplar

Resource Sheet 2: The Leopard Learning Assembly Book

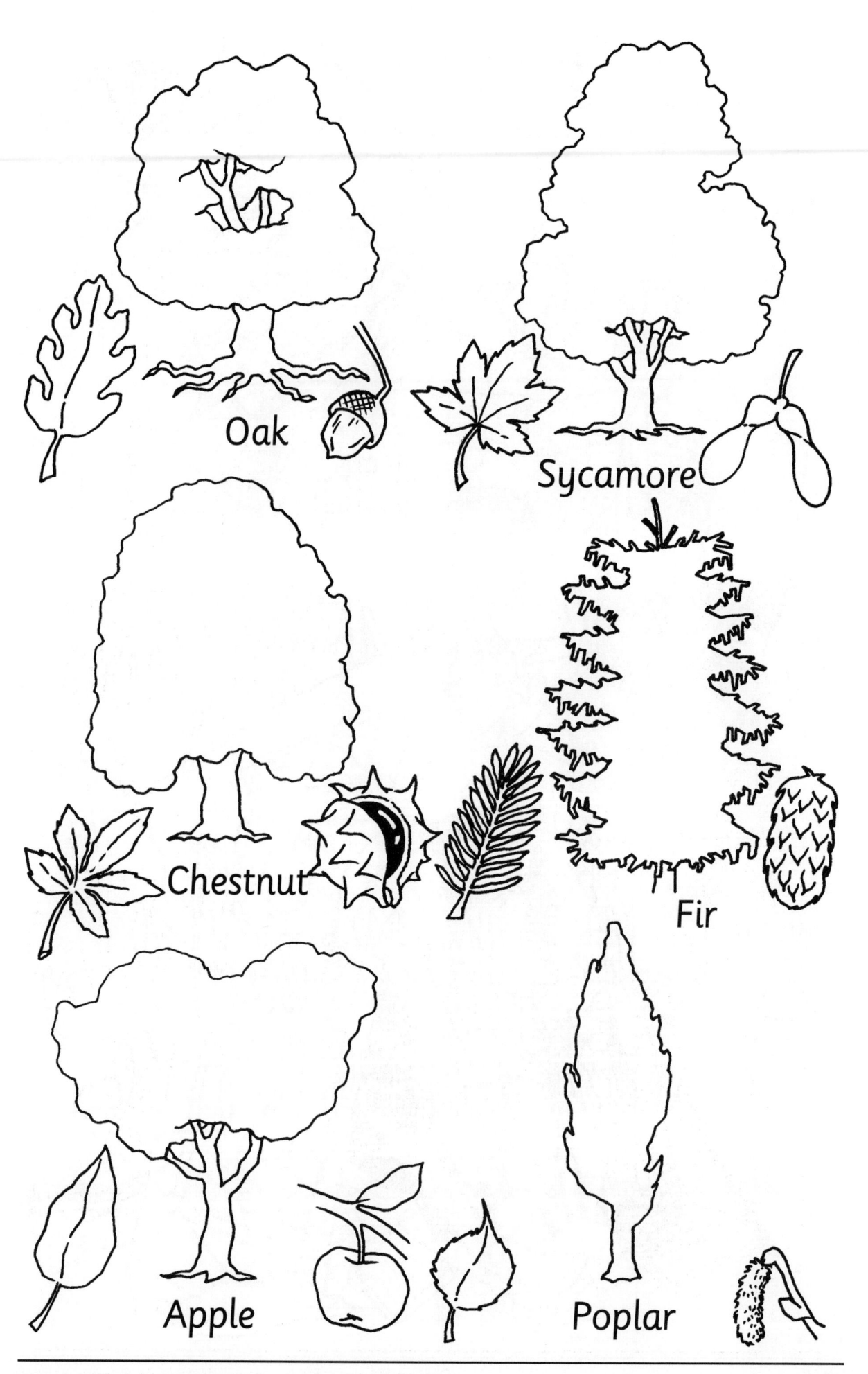

87 Resource Sheet 3: The Leopard Learning Assembly Book

Resource Sheet 4: The Leopard Learning Assembly Book 88

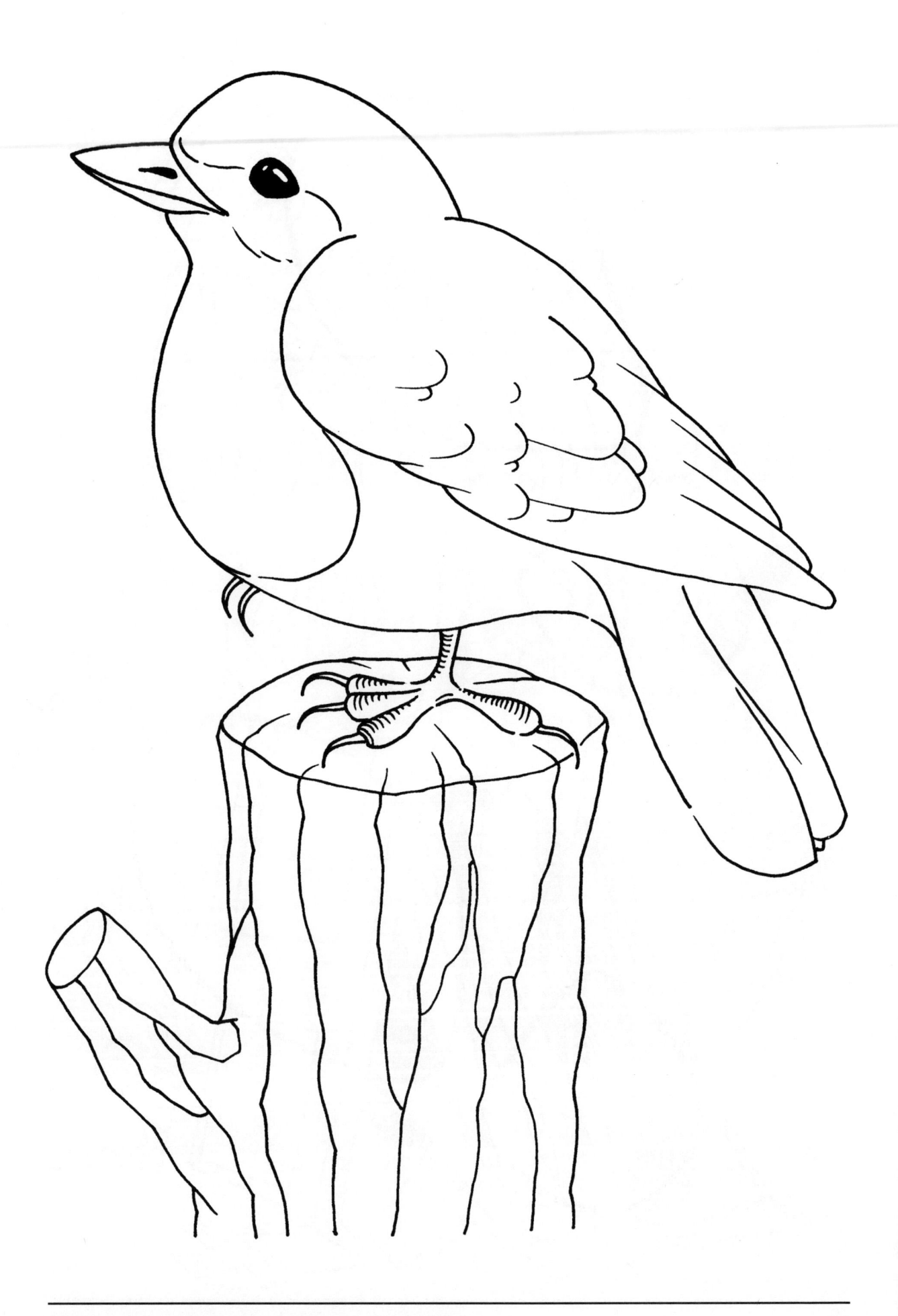

Resource Sheet 5: The Leopard Learning Assembly Book

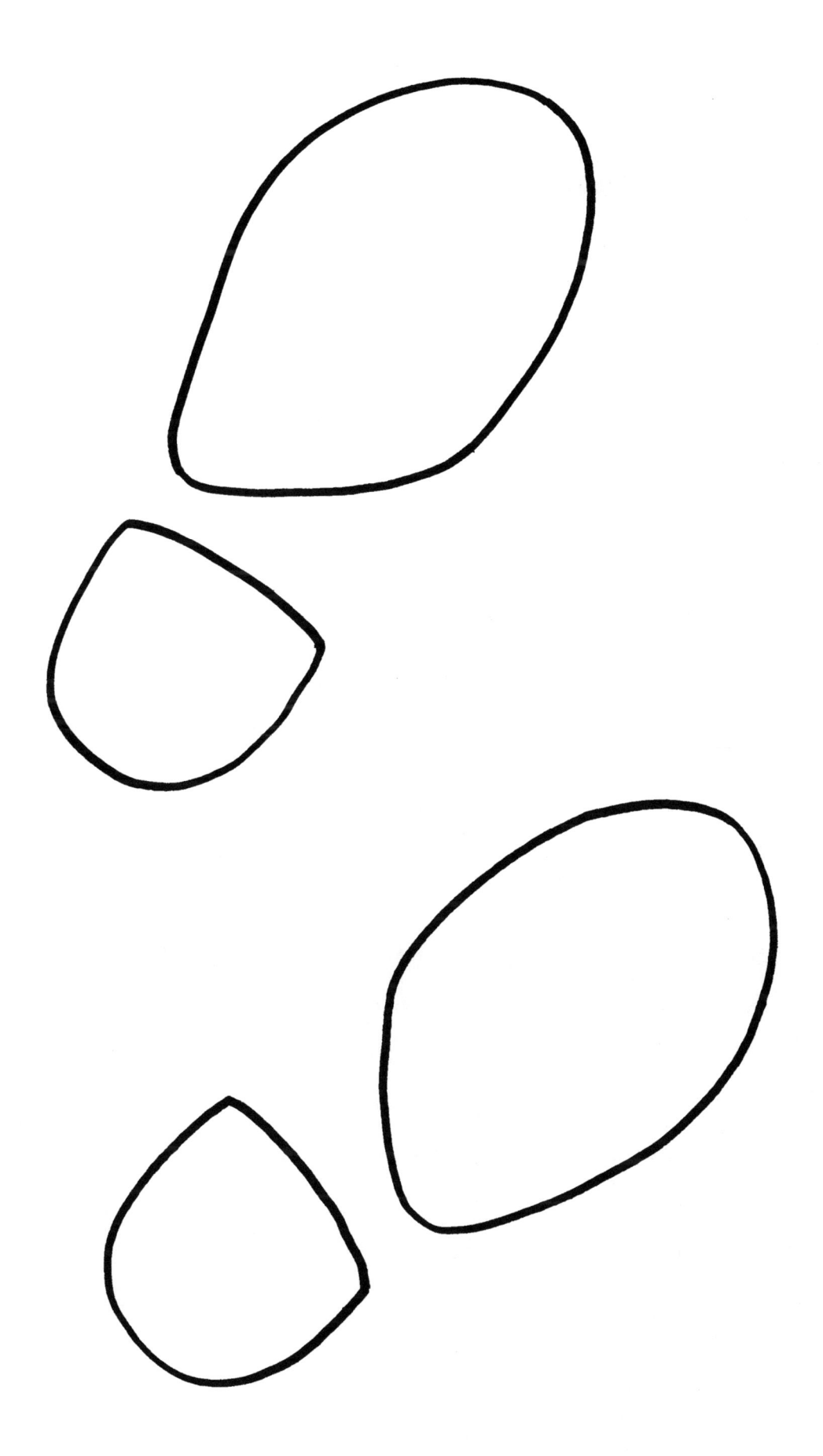

The Christmas Story

Carol 'Once in Royal David's City' - first verse (Junior Praise 185)

Narrator In the little town of Nazareth there lived a young woman called Mary. She was engaged to be married to a man named Joseph who was a carpenter. One day, while Mary was alone she was visited by an angel whose name was Gabriel. The angel said to Mary:

Gabriel I have a special message from God for you, Mary. God has chosen you to have his baby and you will call him 'Jesus'. He will be a king whose reign will never end.

Narrator Mary was very puzzled by this and said to the angel:

Mary How can I have a baby? I am not married to Joseph yet.

Gabriel God's Holy Spirit will come to you. Your baby will be the Son of God.

Narrator Mary told Joseph about the angel Gabriel. Joseph was worried and did not know whether to believe her. Then one night Joseph had a dream in which he saw an angel who told him that Mary's baby was a gift from God. The angel told Joseph to marry Mary and take care of her.

Gabriel The baby will be a little boy whom you must call 'Jesus' which means 'Saviour'.

Resource Sheet 6a: The Leopard Learning Assembly Book

Narrator When Joseph awoke from his dream he told Mary everything the angel had said. Months later, Mary and Joseph were told they must leave Nazareth. The Roman rulers of Israel wanted to find out how many people there were in the country. Everyone had to report back to the town where they were born, to be counted. Mary and Joseph had to go to Bethlehem, where Joseph had been born. Mary rode to Bethlehem on a donkey but Joseph had to walk all the way, by her side.

After several days they arrived in Bethlehem. They were both very tired and knew the baby would be born soon, so they looked for somewhere to stay but people had come from far and wide to be counted. All the inns were full up.

Joseph I wonder, do you possibly have a room we could stay in for the night? My wife is about to have a baby.

Inn keeper I am very sorry, every room is taken but you may spend the night in the stable if you don't mind being with the animals. At least you will be able to keep warm in the straw.

Narrator In the stable that night, baby Jesus was born. Mary and Joseph were overjoyed. They washed Jesus and wrapped him in strips of cloth. Then they tried to find somewhere for Jesus to sleep. All they could find was a feeding box for the animals, called a manger. So they filled the manger with clean straw and put Baby Jesus in it to sleep.

Carol 'Away in a manger'   (Three verses)   (Junior Praise 12)

Narrator In the hills nearby, a group of shepherds were looking after their sheep when the angel appeared to them.

Gabriel Don't be frightened. I have brought you good news. Tonight, the Saviour has been born. You will find him lying in a manger in a stable in Bethlehem.

Carol 'While shepherds watched their flocks by night' (First verse.) (Junior Praise 285)

Narrator The shepherds decided to go straightaway to Bethlehem to see the new born baby for themselves. They found the stable, went inside and saw the baby lying there. The shepherds said:

Shepherds An angel came to tell us that a very special baby had been born so we have come to worship him.

Narrator Sometime after Jesus had been born he was visited by three very wise men.

Wise men We have seen a bright new star in the sky and believe that it is a very special sign. It seemed to lead us all the way here to Bethlehem.

Narrator When they saw Baby Jesus they, too, knelt down and worshipped him. They gave him gifts of gold, frankincense and myrrh.

Carol
'Little Jesus sweetly sleep' (Most carol sheets) 'Silent Night' (Junior Praise 219)

Prayer

(Narrator) Father God, we thank you for your love in sending Jesus as a baby at Christmas time. Thank you that he came to be our Friend and Saviour. As he brings happiness to us, help us, too, to bring joy to others. Amen

Carol
'Hark, the herald angels sing' (Junior Praise 69)

Our carol service

At Christmas time we thank God for his love for us, as shown in the gift of his Son Jesus born many years ago in the stable at Bethlehem.

Carol

'O come all ye faithful' (verses 1 and 5 - 'Sing choirs of angels') (Junior Praise 176)

Reading (From Luke Chapter 1)

The angel Gabriel comes to Mary with good news.

The angel said to Mary, 'Peace be with you...the Lord has greatly blessed you...you will have a son and will name him Jesus...this holy child will be called the Son of God.'

Carol

'Once in royal David's city' (First two verses) (Junior Praise 185)

Reading (From Luke Chapter 2)

The Birth of Jesus

The Roman Emperor Augustus ordered that all the people had to be counted - each person going to his own home town for this purpose. Joseph had to go to Bethlehem because it was the birthplace of King David and he was one of his descendants. He took with him Mary who was having a baby.

Song

'Little donkey, carry Mary' (Carol sheet)

Reading (From Luke Chapter 2)

      Joseph and Mary arrive in Bethlehem.

While they were in Bethlehem the time came for Mary to have her baby. She gave birth to her son, wrapped him in strips of cloth and laid him in a manger because there was no room for them to stay in the inn.

Carol

'Away in a manger' (Junior Praise 12)

Reading (Based on Luke Chapter 2)

      The angels tell the good news to the shepherds.

Some shepherds were spending the night in the fields taking care of their flocks when suddenly an angel appeared to them and said, 'Don't be afraid, I have come to bring good news, today in David's town your Saviour has been born, he is Christ the Lord...you will find the baby wrapped in strips of cloth and lying in a manger'. Then a great number of angels appeared. They were all singing praises to God.

Carol

'While shepherds watched their flocks' (First and last verses) (Junior Praise 285)

Reading (Based on Matthew Chapter 2)

      The Wise Men go to see Jesus

It was when Herod was king in Judea that Jesus was born in Bethlehem. Soon afterwards some wise men came from the east to Jerusalem looking for the baby which had been born. When Herod heard about it he was very upset

Resource Sheet 7b: The Leopard Learning Assembly Book

because he didn't like being told that Jesus was to be a king. Herod's advisers told him that the baby would be in Bethlehem, so the king asked the wise men from the east to search for the child and then report back to him.
The wise men set out on their journey. A very bright star guided them to the place where Jesus was. When they found him they knelt down and worshipped him and presented him with special gifts, gold, frankincense and myrrh. When they came to leave they went back to their own country a different way because God warned them not to go back to Herod.

Carol 'We three kings of Orient are' (Verse one only) (Junior Praise No. 271)

Prayer We give you our thanks Dear Father for your love in sending Jesus at Christmas time to be our Saviour. As the shepherds and the wise men went to worship Jesus, so we too have sung your praises. As they presented their gifts, we too offer ourselves as we promise to follow him and do the things he wants us to do. Amen

Carol Hark the herald angels sing (First verse only.) (Junior Praise No. 69)

The Grace May the peace and love of the Lord Jesus be with each of us this Christmas time and always. Amen

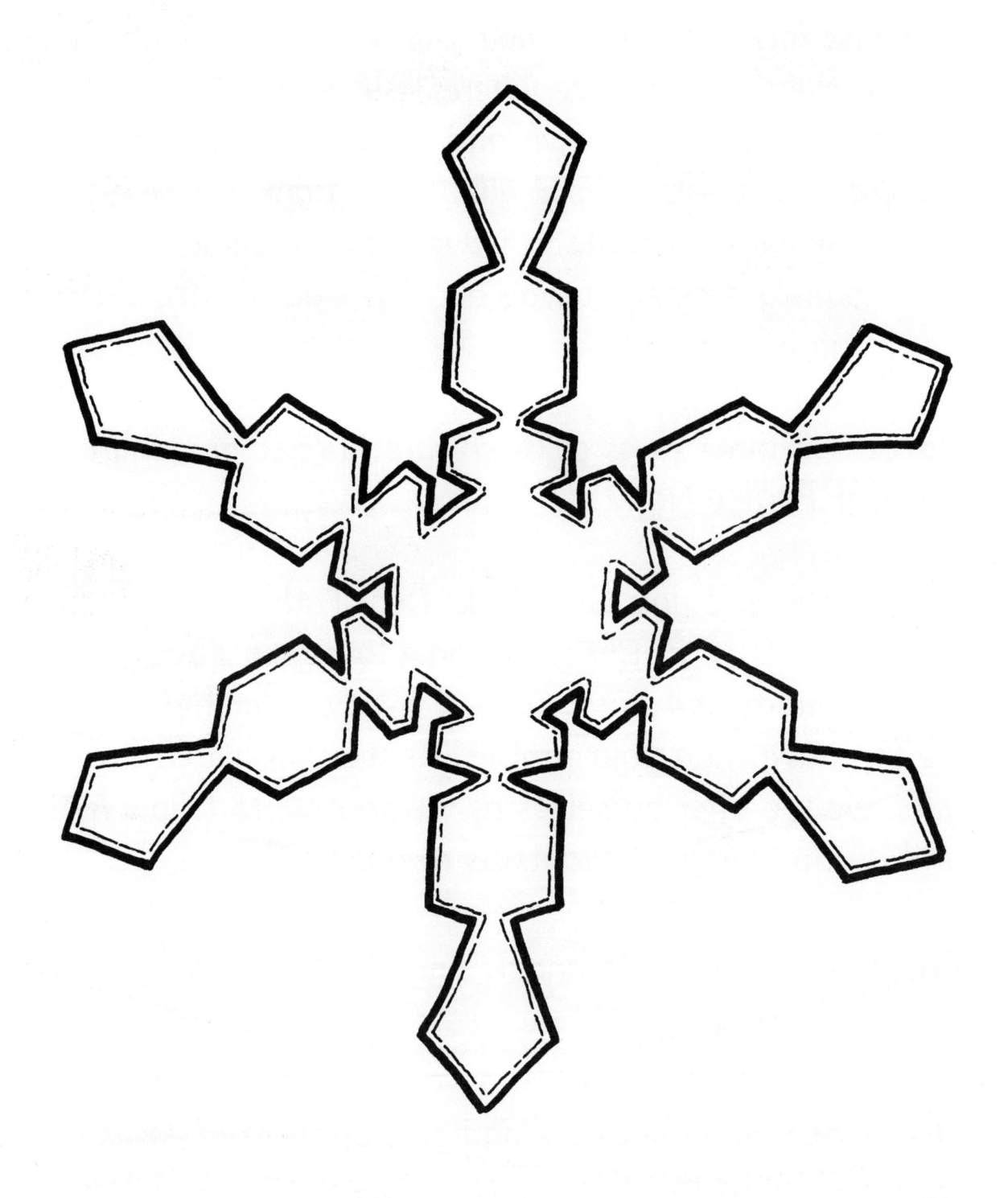

Resource Sheet 8: The Leopard Learning Assembly Book 96

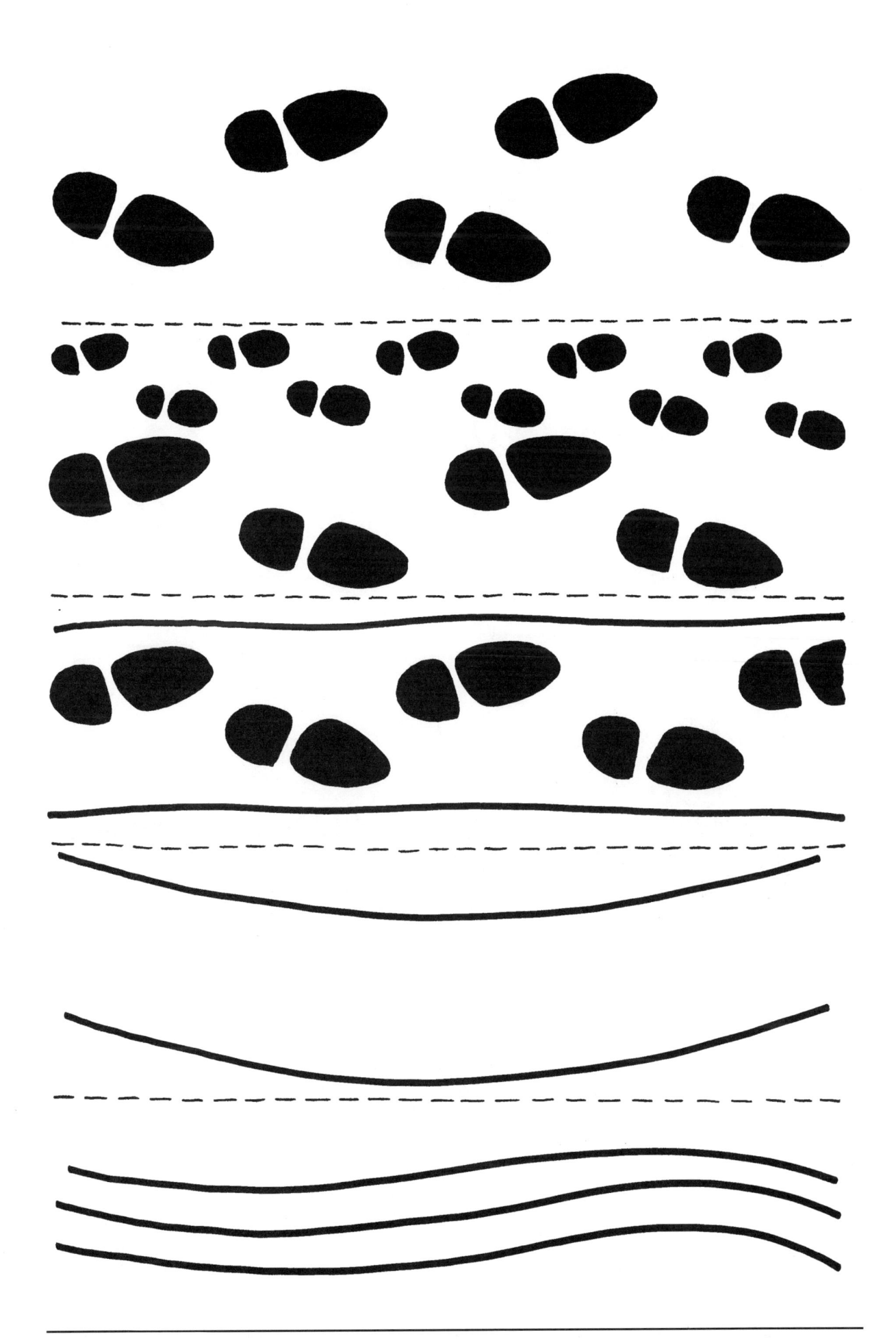

Resource Sheet 9: The Leopard Learning Assembly Book

Mum owes Ali...

1. For keeping his bedroom tidy — 40p
2. For cleaning his own shoes — 40p
3. For doing his piano practice — 80p
4. For washing his hands and face every day. — 80p
5. For being good (Most of the time) — 60p

Total £3·00.

Ali owes Mum...

1. For preparing all his meals - NOTHING
2. For doing all the housework - NOTHING
3. For taking Ali on holiday - NOTHING
4. For buying him new clothes - NOTHING
5. For nursing him when sick - NOTHING

Total - NOTHING

Resource Sheet 10: The Leopard Learning Assembly Book

Resource Sheet 11: The Leopard Learning Assembly Book

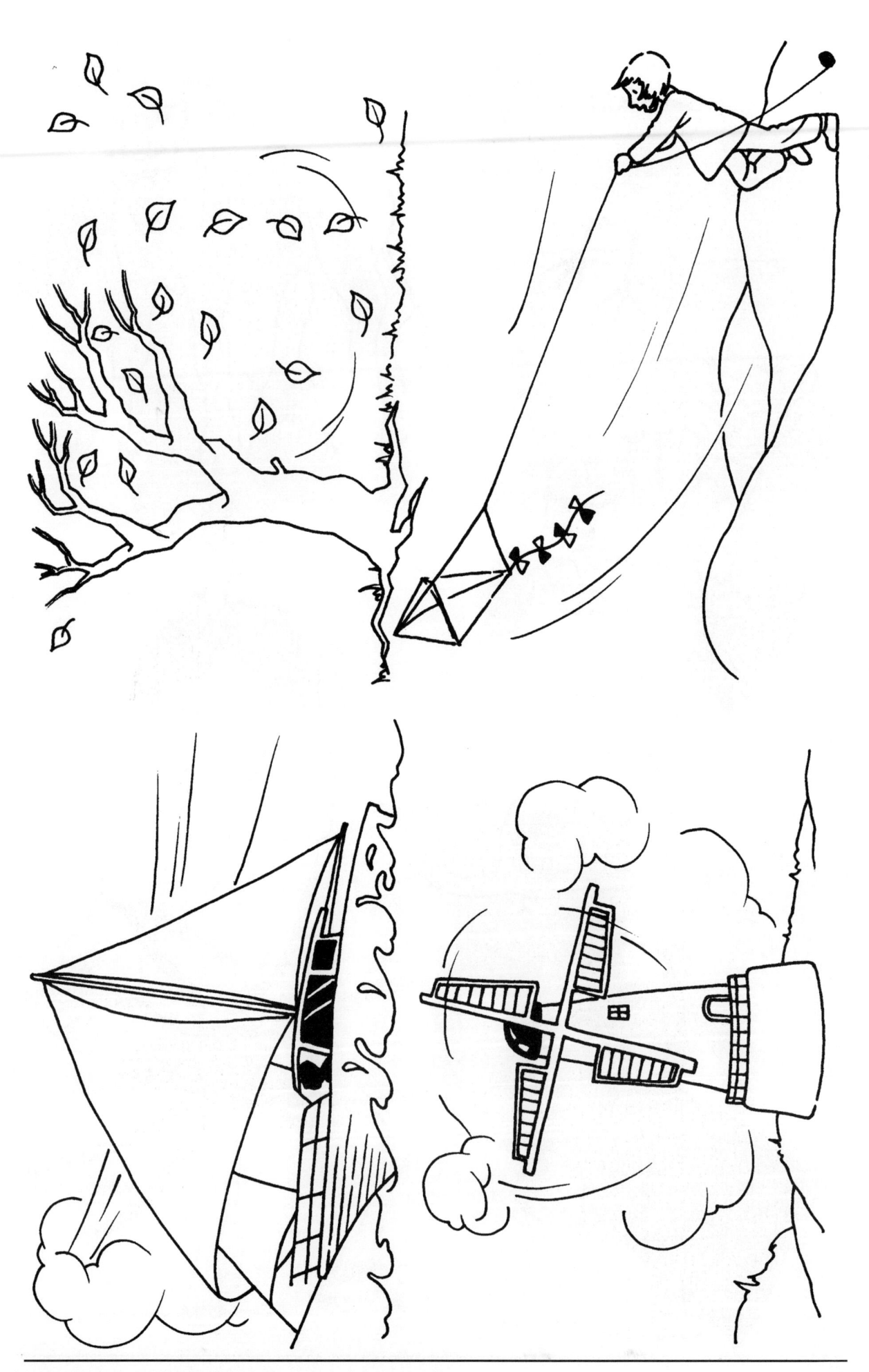

Resource Sheet 12: The Leopard Learning Assembly Book

101 Resource Sheet 13: The Leopard Learning Assembly Book

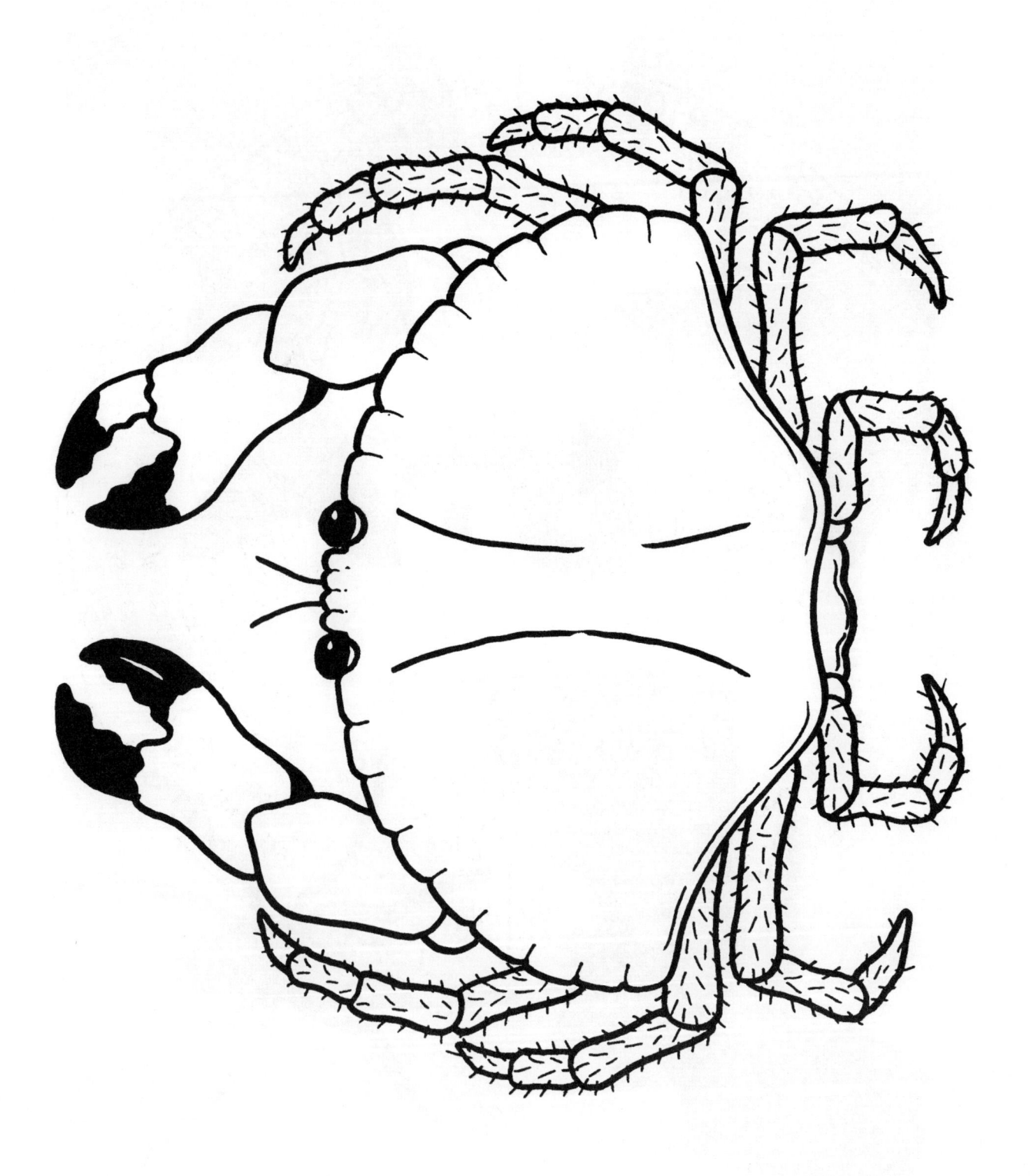

Resource Sheet 14: The Leopard Learning Assembly Book

Resource Sheet 15: The Leopard Learning Assembly Book

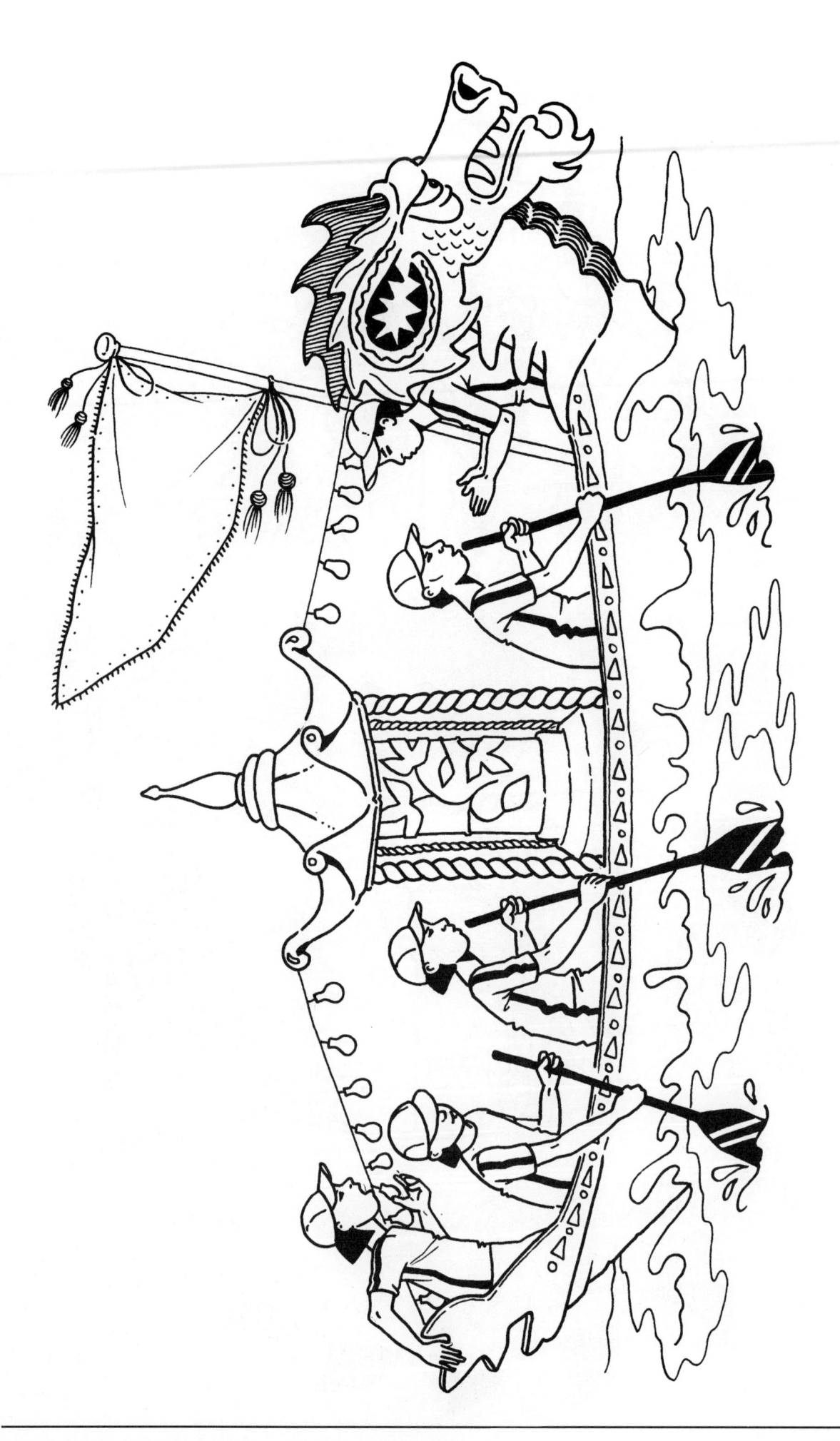

Resource Sheet 16: The Leopard Learning Assembly Book   104

105 Resource Sheet 17: The Leopard Learning Assembly Book

Resource Sheet 18: The Leopard Learning Assembly Book

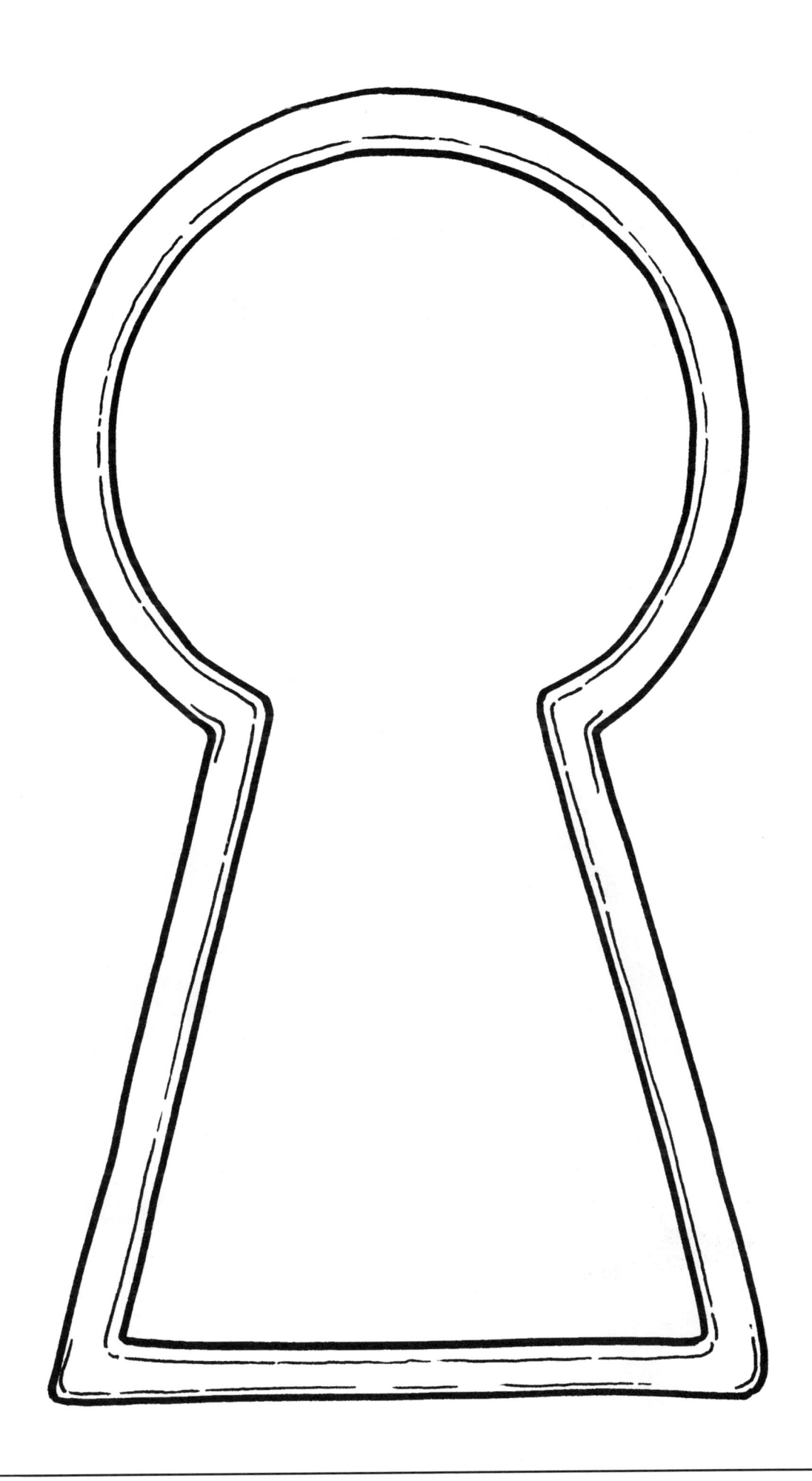

107 Resource Sheet 19: The Leopard Learning Assembly Book

Resource Sheet 20: The Leopard Learning Assembly Book 108

109

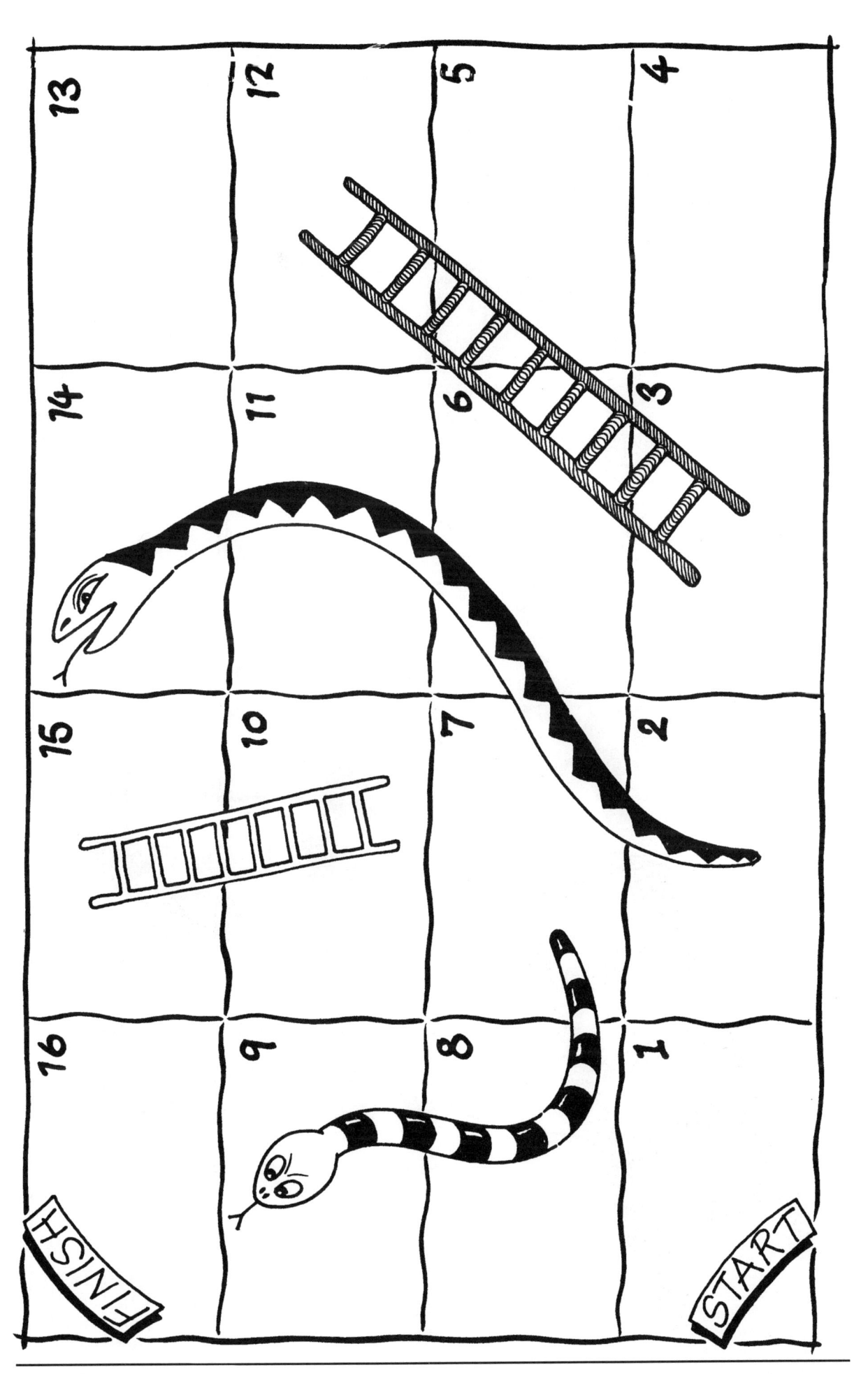

Resource Sheet 21: The Leopard Learning Assembly Book

Resource Sheet 22: The Leopard Learning Assembly Book

Mr Everybody

Mr Somebody

Mr Anybody

Mr Nobody

Resource Sheet 23: The Leopard Learning Assembly Book

There was a crooked man
Who walked a crooked mile,
He found a crooked sixpence
Against a crooked stile.
He bought a crooked cat,
Which caught a crooked mouse
And they all lived together
In a little crooked house

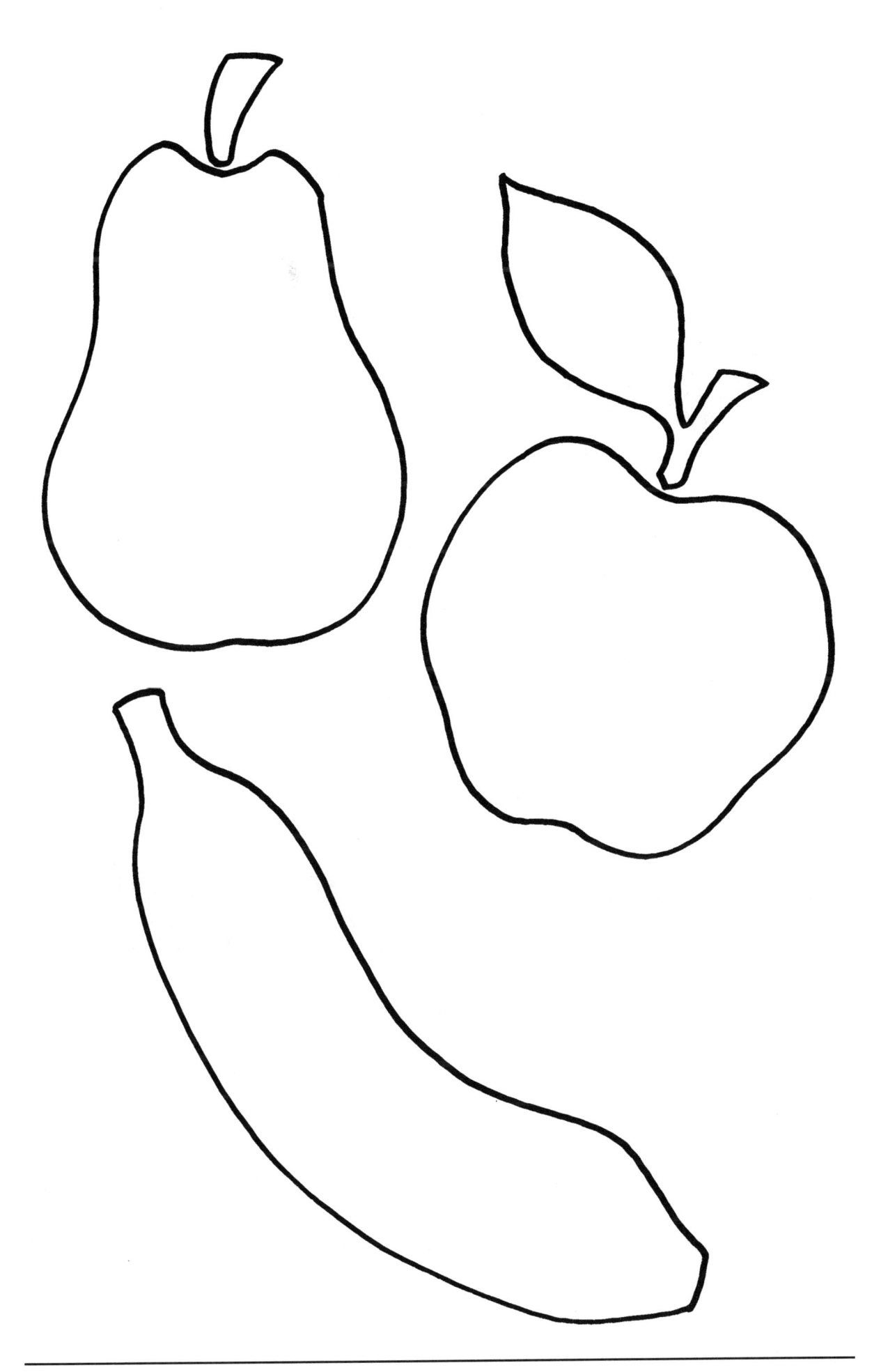

Resource Sheet 25a: The Leopard Learning Assembly Book

Resource Sheet 25b: The Leopard Learning Assembly Book

115 Resource Sheet 26: The Leopard Learning Assembly Book

Resource Sheet 27: The Leopard Learning Assembly Book